Mountain-Moving Motivation

HOW TO EXPERIENCE THE POWER OF GOD!

by Karl Strader
with Stephen Strang

Joy BOOKS

Orlando, Florida 32805

Bible quotations are from the King James Version.

First printing, November, 1978

Portions of this book previously appeared in *Charisma* magazine and *Restoration* magazine.

Joy Books, P.O. Box 2374, Orlando, Florida 32802

Cover design by Nancy Young
Cover photo by Jim Ferrell

To My Wife

It would be difficult to write, preach or do anything without the support of my faithful wife, Joyce.

During the past 24 years, Joyce has contributed much to the part of my life that is poured into this book. We have been through a lot together. We are each very different in a way that complements the other's personality. I'm glad we're different because life would be dull otherwise!

We also help each other be more complete Christians. Joyce gives my ministry a balance it would not have if she were not my wife. I love her more now than I did 24 years ago when we were married.

So I dedicate this, my first book, to Joyce Wead Strader, a woman who is not only my lovely wife, but also my best friend.

Contents

Introduction

Karl Strader has discovered how to move "mountains" in life — through the power of the Holy Spirit. In this book, he tells in his own easy-to-read style how the Holy Spirit can move "mountains" in your life.

This book tells you how the Holy Spirit will deliver you from fear, heal your body, keep you from ever having a blue day, enable you to live a holy life free from sin, and motivate you to witness.

With examples from his own life and ministry, Pastor Strader gives guidelines of how you, too, can experience the mountain-moving power of the Holy Spirit every day of your life.

I have been close personal friends with Pastor Strader for many years. I love him deeply, and am honored to be asked to introduce this, his first book. I have watched his ministry mature and grow until he is, today, one of the leaders of the pentecostal movement and charismatic renewal nationwide.

I have seen him weather storms of life that would

have defeated lesser men. But he was able to draw on the power of the Holy Spirit in his life to move those mountains. Truly, he knows about "Mountain-Moving Motivation!"

Pastor Roy Harthern
Calvary Assembly
Winter Park, Florida

Prologue

When I was a teenager, I worked summers pitching alfalfa hay. I remember that the first few times I jabbed a pitchfork into the freshly mowed hay, I couldn't get any on the fork. The hay was so matted on top I could barely budge it.

An old farmer saw my plight and pointed out I was standing on the hay I was trying to pitch. To my amazement, when I stood back a step or two, I got a fork full of hay with the greatest of ease.

That's like our walk with God. If we will stand back and allow God to work in our lives through the power of the Holy Spirit, we will find it is easy. Even mountains in our lives will move with the greatest of ease.

The reason I wrote this book is that I'm concerned when I see Christians struggling to serve God.

My experience is that by comparison to the sinner, being a Christian is easy. The Word says, "The way of transgressors is hard!" (Prov. 13:15). And it also says, "For my yoke is easy, and my burden is light!" (Matt. 11:30).

MOUNTAIN-MOVING MOTIVATION

The only way the Christian life is possible, let alone easy, is by the Spirit and the power of God. Jesus Christ is the power of God!

Many people try, work, plod and agonize, in their own strength to live for Christ. How fruitless! How discouraging! How unrewarding!

It is never necessary for any Christian to have a blue day. It is never necessary for a Christian to be discouraged. It is never necessary for any Christian to be defeated!

Jesus was a man of sorrows and acquainted with grief but He absolutely was not a man of sadness nor despair.

God wants His children to be on top of the mountain even when they are going through a valley. He wants them to have a song in the middle of the night.

Problems? Sure, Christians will probably have more problems than sinners, because they are going against the current of this world. But a Christian who relies on the power of God flowing through him will never meet a problem with which he cannot cope nor solve. A Spirit-motivated Christian may have to regroup occasionally, but he doesn't know what defeat is, and "retreat" is not in his vocabulary. He is one who always *WINS*, and I mean *EVERY TIME!*

Mountains are strongholds of satanic power. To try to defeat the devil with carnal weapons is like trying to win an atomic war with bows and arrows.

There is only one way to live a victorious Christian life. There is only one way to do any kind of an exploit for God. There is only one way to stand before

Prologue

God one day with the congregation of the righteous.
We must depend totally upon the Spirit of the living
God to give us that *Mountain-Moving Motivation!*

Karl D. Strader
Lakeland, Florida
October 1, 1978

1.
He Saves Us

I vividly recall one night when I was 16, sitting at the top of what we called "Old Vesper Hill," at a youth camp in Western Oklahoma. I was feeling alone, frustrated, and full of despair.

Earlier that day a minister of the Gospel who was attending the camp had looked at me across the breakfast table and told me he didn't see any reason why we should have to believe in the virgin birth. Not long before, another minister had put his long arm around my lanky frame and said, "Son, you don't have to worry about hell." Apparently he didn't, either.

My godly mother taught me about the Lord, and I grew up in a church where old-fashioned preachers preached that the Bible was really true. I thought you could believe preachers. Now, these men of the cloth were causing me to question the veracity of the Bible. I was confused. Things didn't make sense. I wanted to sort them out in my mind, so I had trudged to the top of that lonely hill.

MOUNTAIN-MOVING MOTIVATION

Someone had placed a rough hewn cross there. I flung myself prostrate before it, crying out my inner frustrations to God. I would cry a few minutes, then wait for a vision or some other kind of manifestation to reaffirm my faith. I would have settled for the audible voice of God. But in the stillness of the summer night, all I heard were the sounds of trucks winding their way through the pass in the mountain or the sound of a jukebox at one of the many taverns in the valley far below.

I looked up and gazed at the stars flung against the blackness of the night. I knew heaven was up there somewhere. I visualized how clean and wonderful it must be. Then I looked at the blinking lights in the valley below and knew how wicked most people were. It was as if, at the top of that mountain, I were suspended between heaven and hell.

I lay there for what seemed like hours crying out to God — waiting, weeping, praying, but getting nowhere. It seemed the more I prayed, the more silent He became. Finally, out of sheer desperation, I stood up and began to reason with God as Isaiah had done in the Old Testament days.

"Lord," I began, "I'm not even sure if You're out there! Those old-fashioned preachers I used to hear preach said You're there. I believe they knew what they were talking about. But where are You?"

I reasoned not with my head but with my heart. What my head couldn't understand or wouldn't believe, my heart knew was right. As I continued to pray, a new resolve took shape in my spirit.

"Lord, whether anyone else believes in the virgin

birth or believes there is a hell, I do. Whether anyone else believes the Bible is true, I believe it. Whatever it says, I believe. If it says that I can experience the power of God when I repent of my sins and I believe upon Jesus as my Lord and Saviour, then I believe that, too."

Right there, in the stillness of the night, I surrendered everything to the Lord — my hopes, my ambitions, my adolescent aspirations and dreams. I asked for forgiveness for my doubts, my neglect, my sinning against God. From the depths of my soul I cried out, "Lord Jesus, I'm selling out to you!"

As I prayed, something happened. A peace that passes all understanding flooded my soul, replacing the doubt and frustration I had been feeling. No heavenly baseball bat knocked me out under the power of God. I did not feel the brush of angels' wings. It was the sweet presence of the Lord Himself that quickly but gently enveloped me, filling every fiber of my being. For the first time in my life, I *knew* the power of God was flowing through me.

I thought I was the one who was seeking God that night. Not so. It was the Spirit of God seeking me, drawing me to experience the power of God.

I did not know then what I know now. There is *nothing* one can do by himself to gain an experience with God. The Holy Spirit does the work. The Holy Spirit draws us through repentance. Salvation comes to us through the Lord Jesus Christ, step by step, as the Holy Spirit leads us first to repentance, then to belief, and finally to the new birth.

MOUNTAIN-MOVING MOTIVATION

He Draws Us Through Repentance

The Holy Spirit of God draws us to Jesus through repentance (John 6:44). In other scriptures, we know that He draws us through sorrow, confession and conversion.

Godly sorrow, the scripture says in II Corinthians 7:10, "worketh repentance to salvation, not to be repented of." We must be broken if we are to experience the Power of God. The Holy Spirit convicts us and breaks us. God loves a contrite heart (Ps. 51:17).

Think about the woman who washed Jesus' feet with her tears and dried them with her hair while Jesus ate with Simon the Pharisee. She was truly sorry for her sins, and her tears must have been tears of sorrow. The Bible calls her a sinner, yet Jesus said, "Thy sins are forgiven" (Luke 7:48).

We should be sorry for our sins. After all, it was our filthy jokes, our lies, our rebellion, our subbornness, our uncontrolled appetites, our unbridled lust that nailed Jesus to Golgotha's cross. Each of our sins drove those spikes a little deeper into His hands and feet.

Being sorry is necessary, but it is not enough. We must also *confess* our sins. Three of the most difficult words any of us have ever had to say are, "I was wrong." The Bible says, "If we confess our sins, He is faithful and just to forgive us our sins and to cleanse us from *all* unrighteousness" (I John 1:9).

But confession by itself is not enough either. There must also be a conversion. That is, there must be a turning from the old life to follow Jesus. Our lives must change 180 degrees. Instead of lying, we must be honest. If we hated, we must love. Where there was resentment, there must now be forgiveness.

He Draws Us Through Belief

Paul told the Philippian jailer, "Believe on the Lord Jesus Christ and thou shalt be saved" (Acts 16:31). We must believe to the extent of trusting in Jesus and receiving His Spirit into our hearts. There must be repentance with belief. It is not merely believing, because the Bible says, "the devils also believe and tremble" (James 2:19).

The beautiful thing about belief is that as the Holy Spirit draws us to Himself in repentance, He drops faith into our hearts so that we *can* believe.

When we come to Jesus, we must come just as we are. It does not matter to Jesus whether we were thought to be very wicked before conversion, or if we were considered moral citizens of our communities. Nathanael, for example, was a man in whom Jesus said there was no guile (John 1:47). He was brought to Jesus by Philip. Nathanael believed almost immediately that Jesus was the Messiah, with hardly any proof. He underwent a change of attitude, however, because before believing on Jesus, he had asked if anything good could have come out of Nazareth.

Whether we were wicked or comparatively moral before conversion, there must still be repentance and belief motivated by the Holy Spirit. We must also receive Christ into our hearts as our personal Lord and Saviour.

This Is What We Call The New Birth

New birth is when God's Spirit blends with our spirits and makes our souls come alive. His Spirit even quickens our mortal bodies (Romans 8:11), looking forward to the time when our bodies will be redeemed in the resurrection. This is how it is when the Spirit of God comes into our lives, bringing to us the power of God.

When the new birth takes place, we experience the power of God in our lives for the first time.

Paul experienced it on the road to Damascus. He had been a religious man, exemplary in his Jewish fervor. He was well educated and a devout disciple of what he believed to be right. Most of us know the story of his encounter with God. He was knocked down and blinded by a great light. A voice from heaven said, "Why persecutest thou me?" (Acts 9:4).

"Who art thou, Lord?" Paul cried. Even though he did not know what was going on, Paul recognized that he was speaking to the Lord.

"I am Jesus whom thou persecutest," the Voice answered.

"Lord, what would you have me to do?"

The Lord told him to go to Damascus. There, the Lord showed him in a vision that a man named Ananias would pray for his eyes to be healed. At the same time in another part of town, the Lord told Ananias to pray for Paul. Ananias obeyed. Paul was healed and filled with the Holy Spirit.

Can you imagine the impact on your life that having such an experience would have? It was not only life-changing for Paul, but he had such power with God that he personally evangelized much of the region surrounding the Mediterranean.

My own conversion had a similar impact on my life. That night on Old Vesper Hill something happened inside me as I experienced that power in my spirit. I recognized I had struck fire. When I walked down the hill back to camp, I felt as if I were ten feet tall. I did not shout outwardly. But I was shouting inwardly. Why? Because I had begun to experience the power of God in my life.

What God did for me, He has done for untold multitudes of others throughout church history. God is no respecter of persons. He'll do the same for you. Like the song says, "Though millions have come, there is still room for one." Let that one be you.

When you sense the Spirit of God drawing you, *repent*. When you sense the Spirit of God dropping faith into your heart, *believe*. Then, as you sense the peace of God that passes all understanding welling up within your soul like an artesian well, you can be sure you are experiencing the power of God.

When you sense the Spirit of God, *yield* to that Spirit, and *respond* to that Spirit. You, too, can experience the power of God!

2.

He Strengthens Us

Someone once said that the Christian life is not difficult, it is impossible!

It is true that none of us can live a Christian life in our own strength. But with the power that comes to us at salvation, we can do all things through Christ who *strengthens* us (Phil. 4:13).

Because of this power, the Christian life can be victorious every day. But to be victorious, there are two areas that all Christians need strength in — tests and battles. Tests have to do with our everyday living experiences. Battles are with the evil side of the unseen world — Satan's world, the world of darkness.

I know Christians who feel pretty good on Sunday, but who are depressed much of the week. One day they are on a spiritual mountaintop and the next day they are lying face down in the valley. They don't have the strength to avoid this roller-coaster-type Christian walk from mountaintop to valley and back again, week after week.

There is no reason for these highs and lows. Jesus is the power of God and we need to practice the consciousness of His presence in our daily lives so we can be victorious every moment. This doesn't mean we will never have problems to face or battles to fight. But it does mean that as the power of God flows through our lives, we will have the *strength* to battle the forces of darkness and to cope with the humdrum activities of life without losing the victory where it counts — in our spirits. We can be on the mountaintop spiritually while we are walking through the valley of problems if we continue to rely on the flow of the precious Spirit of God in our lives.

He Strengthens Us In Tests

As believers, we can have power to overcome every test and to endure problems with patience. Paul says in Colossians 1:11, "Strengthened with all might, according to His glorious power, unto all patience and long-suffering with joyfulness..."

Again, in II Corinthians 12:9, 10, Paul writes, "And He said unto me, My grace is sufficient for thee: for my strength is made perfect in weakness. Most gladly therefore will I rather glory in my infirmities, that the power of Christ may rest upon me."

The tests some Christians undergo, however, are self-inflicted. In other words, they bring them on themselves. For example, if a little Christian lady constantly suffers abuses from her unsaved husband who ridicules her, scorns her faith and resists her participation in church, she certainly is undergoing a test.

But if she married him hoping she could lead him

to the Lord after leading him to the marriage altar, she was just asking for problems. She brought this trial on herself. She should never have married him.

Yet even in that situation, the power of God can meet her need. First, the power of God gives her grace to endure the hardships, and since she has already married the rascal, the power of God can enable her to live a godly life in all humility before him so he will be won to the Lord by her righteous life.

Many tests, however, are not our fault. They are a part of God's discipline. They are part of growing up spiritually. The Bible says they do us good.

It's like an athlete training for the Olympics. If he does not endure a little suffering, if his muscles don't get sore, if he doesn't perspire sometimes, he will never excel.

For this reason, God lets us endure tests and trials.

But look at what Paul says. God wants us to *take pleasure* in *every* infirmity, *every* reproach, *every* necessity, *every* persecution and *every* distress (II Cor. 12:10).

Infirmities

Another word for infirmity is weakness. I remember when I was a small boy I was weak and frail, subject to every childhood sickness that came along, including double pneumonia and chronic appendicitis. I remember what pain is. Sometimes I would be walking down the street with my parents when I would double over in unrelenting agony, often unable to straighten up for hours.

After Jesus came into my life, I began to trust

Him. As a result, the power of God began to flow through my life and the weakness and the pain were taken away. As I grew older, God began to bless my life and to help me overcome my weaknesses through the strength that only Christ can give.

Reproaches

Paul also mentioned reproaches. Other words for this are ridicule or scorn. If we have the power of God flowing through our lives, then we can take pleasure in these things.

I remember when I was a teenager, my best friend and I went to youth camp. The emphasis that particular year had been more on having fun, singing secular songs and playing games than it had been on spiritual things. When I was asked to speak at the morning watch, I mentioned that at this camp we were singing songs like "Waltzing Matilda," rather than choruses like "Thank You Lord, For Saving My Soul," as we had in previous years.

My best friend thought that was silly. He began to ridicule me. Before we ate breakfast a short time later, he was asked to lead a song. I will never forget how he looked straight at me with a scornful glare in his eye and began singing "Waltzing Matilda."

He thought I had gone overboard spiritually. He took a stand against me by ridiculing me. Although I forgave him, he never apologized. Our friendship was never the same.

The people who are the closest to us are frequently the ones who kick us the hardest. But the power of God through His Holy Spirit can help us rise above these things. We must keep a sweet spirit and have a forgiving attitude toward everybody. That gives us the strength we need to get through those tests and trials.

Necessities

Another test Paul mentions is necessities or, as we might say today, hardships. In my own life, I have had to undergo hardships. In college for example, I spent seven difficult years, taking a full load of subjects and frequently working two or three jobs at once. I am not exaggerating when I say I had so little money that I couldn't buy an ice cream cone. It was, without a doubt, the boot camp of my life.

But those hardships were the preparation of my life for later experiences. I learned to depend upon God and rejoice in the flow of the Spirit through each new day. I Corinthians 16:13 says, "Watch ye, stand fast in the faith, quit you like men, be strong." I thank God for those times of hardships. I thank Him even more for His Spirit and His grace which flowed through my life to help me keep my sanity.

Persecutions

Paul said, "I take pleasure in persecutions" (II Cor. 12:10). I believe persecutions are God's will for everyone. When the Bible speaks of suffering, it has nothing to do with sickness, but it does have to do with suffering persecution at the hands of both friends and foes.

Peter wrote: "Beloved, think it not strange concerning the fiery trial which is to try you, as though some strange thing happened unto you: But rejoice, inasmuch as ye are partakers of Christ's sufferings; that, when His glory shall be revealed, ye may be glad also with exceeding joy" (I Pet. 4:12, 13).

Oh, he said, "If ye be reproached for the name of Christ, happy are ye; for the spirit of glory and of God resteth upon you: on their part he is evil spoken of, but on your part he is glorified" (I Pet. 4:14).

When we live right, we know we are going to suffer. That's because we are going to be traveling the opposite direction. We are going to be bumping into people who are headed down the broad road to destruction as we go up the road to life.

The Bible says, "for unto you it is given in the behalf of Christ, not only to believe on Him, but also to *suffer* for His sake..." (Phil. 1:29).

Many Christians don't understand this. They appreciate the joy and the presence of the Lord. They get along great when everything is going well. But when they run into problems or suffer as these verses promise they will, they end up in a valley somewhere holding what Harold Hill would call a "pity party" for themselves.

They haven't discovered that the power of God can sustain them through anything. They don't realize that they should "leap for joy" and thank God for the privilege of suffering for Him (Luke 6:23). They should thank Him, too, for the power to have victory during the suffering.

In my walk with the Lord, I've been in situations like this several times. In my early 20's, I received the "left foot of fellowship" from a church of the same denomination in which I grew up. A liberal pastor was sent to the congregation where I was music director. He sized me up as a religious fanatic. Even though I honestly tried to get along with him, he asked the district superintendent to talk with me and tell me to leave. He said I was a "thorn in his side."

That hurt, because the people in that church were confused and dismayed as a result. I forgave that pastor with the help of God's power. The Lord turned the thing around and thrust me into different areas of ministry and into different fellowships that have resulted in the ministry I have today. But it was still a traumatic experience to be asked to leave a church. I was ousted for saying and believing what I thought was right.

Distresses

Paul also says to take pleasure in distresses or difficulties. Several years ago, I was an associate pastor in a midwestern city when a former pastor came to town and started another church. Sixty-five families whom I loved and in whom I had invested part of my life, went to his church.

At the same time, a huge industry in town shut down, and thousands of people, including many in our church, lost their jobs, throwing the entire economy of the area into a recession.

If that wasn't bad enough, the senior pastor had a heart attack. Much of the load of the church was thrown on my shoulders. We, at the same time, were in the middle of a huge building program. Only someone who has been in an experience like that can imagine the pressure. As I look back on it, however, I don't believe I could have coped had it not been for the power of God. While I was in the middle of that situation, it was almost as if I were on tranquilizers because the power of God was so real and so comforting.

I emphasize to the people in our present congregation that the way of the transgressors is hard (Prov. 13:15), but Jesus said, "My yoke is easy and My burden is light" (Matt. 11:30). This doesn't mean the Christian doesn't have problems as perplexing after salvation as before. It does mean, however, that because of the power of God, they don't *seem* as hard. No matter how difficult the load becomes, it doesn't seem that hard because the precious Spirit of God is within us, strengthening us through all kinds of tests.

He Strengthens Us Through Battles

There are other problems we must face that result from attacks of Satan. Paul says in Ephesians 6:12 that, "We wrestle not against flesh and blood, but against principalities, against powers, against the rulers of the darkness of this world, against spiritual wickedness in high places."

The battle we have with Satan is a fight to the finish. But you and I never have to lose! Sometimes the battle is delayed, or we have to regroup. But we never lose if we depend upon the power of God to help us.

More than one-third of the ministry of Jesus had to do with battling the forces of Satan. Many of the people who came to him for healing had a "spirit of infirmity" (Luke 13:11), or a "deaf spirit" (Mark 9:25), and so forth. In these cases, it was more than just a matter of sickness. These were problems in the spiritual realm.

Jesus met others in His ministry who were totally uncontrollable. The Gadarene demoniac, for example was so wild he had to be chained to tombs. Jesus cast a "legion" of demons out of that man. A legion of Roman soldiers included 3,000 to 6,000 foot soldiers. If there were that many evil spirits in the man, no wonder he was troubled. But after Jesus cast the evil spirits out, the man was perfectly sane, totally delivered.

Understanding this battle against Satan is so important that I have devoted the next chapter to discussing it. I tell how we can win the battle against Satan in our own lives.

The Bible says to, "fight the good fight of faith, lay hold on eternal life, whereunto thou art also called" (I Tim. 6:12). Paul tells us what to do when we battle Satan: "Put on the whole armour of God, that ye may be able to stand against the wiles of the devil" (Eph. 6:11).

Jesus gave us the perfect blueprint for how to cope with Satan.

You will recall that Jesus was tempted by Satan when He fasted for 40 days in the wilderness. Some Bible scholars believe that was the only time Jesus had to battle Satan. I believe He battled Satan many times, just as we have to.

For example, when Peter tried to tell Jesus He didn't have to go to the cross, Jesus saw who was behind what Peter was saying, and He commanded Satan, "Get thee behind me!" (Matt. 16:23).

He also battled the evil one when He commanded the devils to come out of the man from the country of the Gadarenes and when he prayed so hard in the Garden of Gethsemane that He sweat great drops of blood.

Since Jesus had to battle Satan, too, we should cope with Satan the same way He did.

Jesus' Formula For Battling Satan

1. First, Jesus was filled with the Spirit. He had just come from being baptized in water by John the Baptist and the Spirit of God had descended on Him (Luke 3:21, 22).

2. Jesus fasted and prayed. There are certain demonic problems, Jesus told His disciples one time, that are dealt with only after fasting and praying (Mark 9:29).

3. Jesus quoted scripture when Satan tempted Him. He had the Word of God hidden in His heart. He used the Word against satanic foes (Luke 4:4, 8, 12).

4. Finally, Jesus knew how to take His authority as a believer. He commanded the devil to leave Him alone. He wasn't timid when it came to telling Satan where to go (Matt. 4:10).

The scripture says, "There hath no temptation taken you, but such as is common to man: but God is faithful, who will not suffer you to be tempted above that you are able; but will with the temptation make a way to escape, that ye may be able to bear it" (I Cor. 10:13). The Bible makes it plain that the power that is in us is greater than the power that is in the world (I John 4:4). If we will allow the power of God to flow through our lives, we will have victory. We will win every time!

3.
He Delivers Us

Every Christian must cope with attacks of one kind or another from the enemy. John 10:10 says, "The thief (Satan) cometh not, but for to steal, and to kill, and to destroy: I (Jesus) am come that they might have life, and have it more abundantly."

That is the key. When we are attacked by Satan, we must look to Jesus for deliverance so that we might enjoy life "abundantly." There is no way to free ourselves from the power of the enemy except through the power of Jesus Christ and His Holy Spirit. If you don't read any further in this chapter, you will have grasped its essence if you understand that it is the power of God that delivers us!

My understanding of Satan and his work is that all evil in the world comes from him. Sin, sickness, fear — anything evil — has as its source, the devil. As I analyze the scriptures, I do not see as much difference as many Christians seem to make between the works of the flesh and the works of the devil. But what are the works of the devil?

MOUNTAIN-MOVING MOTIVATION

Look at Ephesians 2:1-3: "And you hath he quickened, who were dead in trespasses and sins; Wherein in time past ye walked according to the course of this world, according to the prince of the power of the air, the spirit that now worketh in the children of disobedience: Among whom also we all had our conversation in times past in the lusts of our flesh, fulfilling the desires of the flesh and of the mind; and were by nature the children of wrath, even as others."

Now, notice this! "For this purpose the Son of God was manifested, that He might *destroy* the works of the devil" (I John 3:8). This passage is unmistakably speaking about *sin* indicating that Satan is its source.

But there is another work of the devil. Peter declared to Cornelius and his household, "Jesus of Nazareth ... went about doing good, and healing all that were oppressed of the devil!" (Acts 10:38). The context is referring to *sickness!* (When I refer to sickness, I do not include handicaps or weaknesses.) So both sin and sickness have as their source, Satan!

Based on these scriptures, I believe that behind every sinful, unholy trait and behind every sickness *there is a sinister power of hell.* This does not mean that every unholy trait or every disease is caused by a spirit that needs to be cast out. It does mean, however, that every sinful, unholy trait and or sickness is caused by an evil supernatural power we call Satan.

For example, if a Christian had a problem quitting the cigarette habit he had before he was saved, that dirty habit has as its root, Satan. The Bible teaches that he can be delivered by the power of God. I won't argue whether the devil is *in* him, *on* him or just tormenting him. The devil should be disposed of in the name of Jesus.

We call this "deliverance," because Jesus can *deliver* us from the power of Satan. Thousands of people can testify to being delivered from the cigarette habit, alcoholism, drug addiction, sicknesses of every description, as well as problems of pride, fear, rejection and lust. No matter what the problem is, we have authority through the power of God to make the enemy flee in the name of Jesus.

There are many methods to obtain deliverance, just as there are many methods to witness for Jesus. Later in this chapter, I will give some guidelines for getting rid of *any* sin or sickness.

But first, let's examine the five areas in which Satan attacks us — temptation, oppression, depression, obsession and possession.

Every believer is attacked in the areas of temptation and oppression. Even Jesus was tempted and oppressed of the devil. But you never read anywhere that Jesus was depressed, obsessed and possessed. Christians who find themselves troubled in those areas have allowed Satan to take advantage of them and are not in tune with heaven and with God.

Let's look at these five areas one at a time.

He Delivers Us From Temptation

The power of God can deliver us from temptation. After He received the Holy Spirit, Jesus was tempted in the wilderness to turn the stones into bread, to cast himself off the temple and to fall down and worship Satan. As we discussed in the last chapter, however, He was full of the Holy Spirit. He had also fasted and He used the Word of God to combat the temptations that Satan sent His way.

Jesus taught His disciples to pray every day: "Lead us not into temptation, but deliver us from evil" (Matt. 6:13). If we pray this in faith, the power of God can help us avoid much of the temptation that comes our way. However, we won't avoid all temptation. James said, "Count it all joy when ye fall into divers temptations" (Jas. 1:2). But if we are led by the Spirit of God, He can lead us away from much of it and deliver us from the rest of it.

You see, sometimes we may yield to temptation, and it becomes a torment so that it is a constant root of evil.

In my own life, I have been delivered from the problem of losing my temper and being prejudiced toward others.

I am not proud to admit this, but my parents were members of the Ku Klux Klan. As I grew up, I became prejudiced against blacks, Catholics and Jews.

As a youth, I also had a terrible temper that I constantly battled. I knew I should not lose my temper. I knew being prejudiced was wrong. But these were torments I could not control.

One time an old-fashioned preacher preached sanctification at our church. He said if we would come forward, God would "sanctify us." I understand the terms deliverance and sanctification to be synonymous in many ways. Do you know that the problem with my temper disappeared and that I lost the prejudice I felt toward others? I believe I was delivered of those problems that night at an old-fashioned altar in Western Oklahoma.

Since that time, I have not even been *tempted* to lose my temper. And, I am not *tempted* to be prejudiced. In fact, today I have many dear friends who are black, many who are Catholic and many who are Jewish.

I believe God can deliver us from any problem we might have like this. The power of God can help us to rid ourselves of any unholy traits that might attach themselves to us.

He Delivers Us From Oppression

The power of God also delivers us from oppression. I understand oppression comes in three areas: sickness, harassment and persecution.

Sickness

Sickness is something all of us must cope with sooner or later, even if it is only the common cold. As I stated before, I believe all sickness is from Satan. There was no sickness in the world before Adam and Eve sinned in the Garden of Eden. Sickness, like death, is the result of that fall. When sickness occurs, we must fight against it and believe God to deliver us from it.

A story about my dad will prove a point here. When he was 55 years old, he was given up by the doctors to die. I knew that God had promised us 70 years. I don't believe it is God's perfect will for any of his children to die *sick*. We must all die sooner or later, but we don't have to die because of sickness.

We can die of old age.

While my father was so critically ill, I remembered that King Hezekiah in the Old Testament had prayed for 15 more years to live. So I prayed for 15 more years for my dad. I did not know at the time that I was battling the forces of hell for my father's life and health. But today I understand that is what I was doing.

God heard my prayer. Satan was defeated. My father recovered. He lived 15 more years, then passed away at age 70.

"Is any sick among you? let him call for the elders of the church; and let them pray over him, anointing him with oil in the name of the Lord: And the prayer of faith shall save the sick, and the Lord shall raise him up; and if he have committed sins, they shall be forgiven him. Confess your faults one to another, and pray one for another, that ye may be healed. The effectual fervent prayer of a righteous man availeth much" (James 5:14, 15, 16).

When we get sick, we are oppressed by the enemy. We must pray in faith, that is, in the power of God. (Remember that faith is a Spirit — the Holy Spirit — which is the power of God. II Cor. 4:13). If we do, our prayers will be answered. We can be delivered of whatever illness we have! Frequently this happens because the gifts of healing or miracles are manifested. But it will happen every time when we meet all of the scriptural conditions.

Harassment

The power of God delivers us from harassment. Satan goes about like a roaring lion, the Bible says, "seeking whom he may devour." Most Christians stop there. The passage (I Peter 5:8, 9) goes on to say, "whom resist steadfast in the faith." In other words, don't put up with that harassment. Take authority over the devil and put him to flight!

In the last chapter I wrote about how I was an associate pastor several years ago at a church where the pastor of the church suffered a heart attack. While he was recuperating, I suffered intense pain in my own chest. Sympathy pains? I wasn't sick; it was just an attack of the enemy. The pain didn't leave until I began to rebuke Satan and his power.

Since then, I have had opportunity to take authority over Satan many times when he began to harass me, my family or my ministry. If I only try to suffer quietly, or to change my mental attitude about the problem or to rationalize the problem away, the harassment continues. But when I command Satan to leave in the name of Jesus the harassment stops almost immediately.

The Bible says, "Many are the afflictions of the righteous: but the Lord delivers him out of them all" (Ps. 34:19). Hallelujah. I am thankful that as a Christian, I have the privilege to rebuke Satan in the name of Jesus, and he *must* leave me alone.

Persecution

The third area of oppression is persecution. Some Christians believe that if they serve Jesus everything will always be wonderful, and that no one will ever offend them. That is not what the Bible says.

I have already discussed some of the things I have suffered in the last chapter. I have noticed that most of the situations I have faced have been at the hand of Christians rather than unbelievers.

Many Christians who are otherwise loving and kind, get very belligerent when anyone crosses their traditional way of doing things. Traditions often become more important to them than the scripture itself. When you cross them on tradition, or even on a little different interpretation of scripture, all hell breaks loose. When this happens, I believe it is the enemy seeking to cause disunity.

For seven years I attended a conservative ultra-fundamentalist college that does not believe in any form of ecumenism. A few years after I graduated, I joined the Assemblies of God, a pentecostal denomination. I have also been active in the charismatic renewal which has taken place in main-line denominational churches.

Some time ago a picture was taken of me at a charismatic conference with a group of brethren from Roman Catholic, Episcopalian, Methodist and various other church backgrounds. The photograph was later published. When some people at my alma mater saw it, they decided I had gone too far. Not only did they not endorse the charismatic renewal, but they didn't agree with my associating with people from "liberal" denominations, even though these people were all fellow-believers with a born-again experience.

The college president wrote me a letter which said basically that the college had disowned me. It did not matter that I had attended the college for seven years and that I had a good academic and citizenship record. Because I didn't share the school's view, I was asked never to tell anyone I had attended the college. I believe this was an attack which was initiated by the enemy.

The Bible commands us to bless those who persecute us, and to do good to those who despitefully use us (Matt. 5:44). If we do, and if we keep sweet in our spirits, God will deliver us by His power — even out of persecution.

Up to now we have discussed actions of Satan with which all believers must cope. There are three other types of attack — depression, obsession or possession.

He Delivers Us From Depression

Isaiah 61:1-3 is a beautiful scripture that promises deliverance. "The Spirit of the Lord God is upon me;" Isaiah wrote, "because the Lord hath anointed me to preach good tidings to the meek; he hath sent me to bind up the broken-hearted, to proclaim liberty to the captives, and the opening of the prison to them that are bound; to proclaim the acceptable year of the Lord, and the day of vengeance of our God; to comfort all that mourn; to appoint unto them that mourn in Zion, to give unto them beauty for ashes, the oil of joy for mourning, the garment of praise for the spirit of heaviness; that they might be called trees of righteousness, the planting of the Lord, that he might be glorified."

Let's look at depression; There is no reason for any Christian to be depressed. Even if we are going through a valley, we should not be depressed. Depression is of Satan. We can overcome depression with the power of God.

I praise God that I am seldom blue, lonely, sad or fearful. It has not always been so. At one time in my life I was consumed with fear in a way that left me constantly blue or depressed.

Fear is a terrible thing. Fear is one cause of depression. I believe fear is of Satan. I can remember precisely how fear entered me, and how it left.

Years ago my aunt took us children to a movie every Saturday night in a town six miles away. We rode in the back of her black pick-up truck. The older children thought it was great fun. We saw Dick Tracy thrillers and horror movies with vampires and other creatures. I was too young to handle it. I remember being all shriveled up like a little ball on that theater seat, scared almost to death.

The problem was that the fear stayed with me. At night I would hallucinate. I would see apparitions and every kind of frightening imagination. Many nights I would awaken the entire family with my screaming. This fear continued with me into my teenage years. I was afraid of everything — especially the dark.

One night I had a particularly horrible nightmare. I screamed and screamed. My father came into my room and prayed that Jesus would take away the fear from his son's life. My father was a Christian, but he didn't understand much about the delivering power of the Holy Spirit. In fact, I don't recall ever hearing him pray out loud before that. But that night, he really "got hold of God," as the old-timers would say. He clasped my hand and put his arm around my trembling frame as we knelt by the side of my bed.

"Dear God," he prayed, "I want my boy to be free from this fear."

We agreed together in prayer. I do not know if we realized we were "agreeing" as I would understand it today. I am sure we did not understand that we were battling Satan and the kingdom of darkness. All we knew was that the fear that had depressed me was a terrible thing. We knew that God could somehow remove it.

Praise God He did. I was completely freed of the unnatural fear I had. From that day to this, I have not been tormented by fear. I was delivered. Set free!

The interesting thing about my experience was that we didn't follow the usual formula prescribed by many people in today's "deliverance ministries." We did not understand what we were doing. But the freedom that resulted — the victory that became mine — was valid. It was real. Deliverance worked.

I think this proves there are many ways to experience deliverance. I said earlier that I believe sanctification and deliverance are the same in many ways. It does not matter what we call it as long as we are winning the battle against Satan in our lives, through the power of God. I am not dogmatic about terminology, or even methods. But I am dogmatic about the experience of deliverance and the fact that people can be set free by the power of God!

Because I battled fear in my own life, I am particularly sensitive to this problem in the lives of other people. I estimate that at least one third of all

Christians battle fear of one kind or another. Some are afraid of what other people will think; or, they are afraid of heights, airplanes, water, or small closed-in places. Fear is so common that the word "phobia" which means "fear" in Greek has become a common English word.

It is important to remember there is a natural fear that all of us must have. This type of fear is healthy because it helps us to be cautious on the free-way, careful with electricity, and collected in case of a severe storm. But any *unnatural* fear is of Satan. This type of fear paralyzes us, makes us turn pale, and causes us to do ridiculous things.

Some people have a tremendous fear of speaking before a crowd of people. But the mighty Baptism in the Holy Spirit gives even the most timid people a holy boldness!

Paul writes to Timothy that "God has not given us a spirit of fear; but of power, and of love, and of a sound mind" (II Tim. 1:7).

In a prayer line one time a young man confided in me that he was constantly harassed with homosexual desires. He said he had never committed a homo-sexual act, but he was constantly tormented by the thoughts.

"I know this torment is of the devil," he said. "Can you help me?"

I prayed with him. We agreed together that Satan would be defeated. He confessed it. He renounced it. He resisted it. And he was delivered of it! As far as I know, he has not been harassed with those thoughts since.

44

If we have a hang-up like an overwhelming desire for overeating, smoking, sexual perversion, or whatever — it is demonic in origin. I believe these problems should be dealt with by *daily* taking up our cross to follow Jesus (Luke 9:23).

Let me explain "taking up our cross." That is not the cross of Jesus. He has already paid for our sin. But, as I understand it, it is taking up our *own* cross — the crucifixion of our flesh.

Now, "the body without the spirit is dead" (crucified) (James 2:26). If we get rid of the evil influence of the spirit of lawlessness then we are dead to sin and alive to God!

He Delivers Us From Obsession

Next, we can also be free of obsession. II Timothy 2:26 gives us a picture of what can happen to certain people: "And that they may recover themselves out of the snare of the devil, who are taken captive by him at his will." This means that people can be totally preoccupied with various kinds of evil thoughts and desires.

This is what takes place with people who feel compelled to seek out hard-core pornography. After awhile, what they see is not lurid enough, and they must see grosser forms of perversion to satisfy their twisted desires.

Some people are obsessed with the desire for hard drugs. It is more than just a physical desire. Thousands of people in this country must steal and kill to get enough money to support their drug habits.

Other people are obsessed with the desire to drink;

others are obsessed with food. Whatever the obsession is, it is of the devil.

I vividly recall my first experience with someone who was obsessed with lust. A young man came to my office one day for counseling. Even though he was married and had more than normal sexual relations with his wife, he masturbated two or three times a day and was consumed with lust.

As he talked about his problem the gift of discerning of spirits began to operate in my life. I said: "That is an unclean spirit."

The young man desperately wanted to be free of this obsession. I told him he had to ask God for forgiveness. He prayed, oh, how he prayed, for God to restore the fellowship he once had with Him.

Then I commanded the unclean spirit to leave. To my utter amazement, the young man fell out of his chair and began to writhe like a snake on my office floor. A deep, gutteral voice growled, "I will not come out!" The Spirit showed me that was not a human voice I was hearing.

"You will come out, in the name of Jesus!" I said.

"You can't make me! I will not!" the voice responded.

Then the pupils of the young man's eyes narrowed to slits as though he were on heavy drugs. His mouth began to foam and the voice growled, "I'll kill you."

"I'm not afraid because I'm protected by the blood of Jesus," I declared. "Now, out, in the name of Jesus."

Nothing happened. On and on this went for nearly two hours. I had never experienced anything like it before. I was shaken to the very core of my being. During this time the young man would come to himself for awhile and then begin to utter all kinds of threats and obscenities. Finally I decided to suggest that the young man get help from the evangelist who was holding meetings in our church that week. The evangelist had been accustomed to dealing with evil spirits. He had been fasting and praying. I had not. I felt he would be better equipped to handle it.

That night at the close of the meeting the young man went to the front of the church for prayer. I had not told the evangelist anything about what had taken place in my office. When he came to pray for the young man, however, the evangelist looked at him a minute, through the gift of discerning of spirits he knew what the problem was. "You unclean spirit, come out in the name of Jesus."

It was as if the young man had been shot. He slid to the floor and lay perfectly still like a dead man for about 45 minutes. When he got up his entire countenance had changed. He was free ... totally free! He began to praise God for his deliverance.

Let's discuss the final and most serious area of demonic activity — possession.

He Delivers Us From Possession

One of the best examples of possession is in the story of the Gadarene demoniac whose total depravity is described in Mark 5:1-20. This man was so crazy that he lived among the tombs. He was so wild that people could not even chain him up. He spent his time night and day, the Bible says, crying and cutting himself with stones. In other words, this man was so totally controlled and possessed by Satan that he could not control himself, nor could he be controlled by others.

When Jesus came by, the man ran to Him and worshipped Him. He *asked for help.* But the demons in him cried out with a loud voice, "What have I to do with thee, Jesus, thou Son of the most high God? I adjure thee by God, that thou torment me not."

When Jesus commanded the evil spirits to leave, they pled to be sent into a nearby herd of swine rather than to be sent to a far country. Jesus allowed them to go into the swine, which immediately ran down a steep bank and drowned themselves in the sea.

By the time the word got out what had happened, and a crowd had gathered, the man who had been so depraved was clothed and was sitting quietly at the feet of Jesus.

Satanic possession is a serious and frightening thing. Sadly, many people open themselves up to demonic possession by becoming involved in transcendental meditation, yoga, horoscopes, fortune telling, palm reading, seances, and other forms of divination. This gives the devil an open door to bring in his depression, his obsession, and finally his possession.

Here Is How To Come Against Attacks From Satan

When we are up against Satan and the forces of hell, how can the power of God deliver us? I have a formula which I use, which is effective. I know that it works because it comes from the Word of God.

This is applicable to any of the last three areas of Satanic activity — depression, obsession or possession. Also the same principles can be applied to overcome temptation and oppression in a more general sense not involving actual sin.

1. Confess the problem. I John 1:9 says, "If we confess our sins, he is faithful and just to forgive us our sins, and to cleanse us from all unrighteousness."

2. Renounce it. II Corinthians 4:2 makes it plain that we must renounce the hidden things of dishonesty, which some Bible commentaries call "the shameful things."

3. Count yourself dead to it. Romans 6:11 says, "Reckon ye also yourselves to be dead indeed unto sin." This means to picture in your mind that you are absolutely free from every shackle, every chain, every bondage of Satan. God has given us an imagination which Satan sometimes uses for his benefit. We need to use it to "reckon" (imagine) ourselves dead to whatever the problem is.

4. Command it to go. Many people are harassed by the devil because they do not know they can, as Christians, command him to go in the name of Jesus. God wants us to take authority over the roaring lion who wants to devour us. If we command him to go, "whom resist steadfast in the faith" (I Pet. 5:9), he will go in the name of Jesus.

5. Plead the blood of Jesus. Revelation 12:11 says, "And they overcame him (Satan) by the blood of the Lamb, (Jesus) and by the word of their testimony." When we say we "plead the blood" or we are "covered by the blood" it means we plead for the protection (or we are covered with the protection of God) *because of the blood* Jesus shed on Calvary. As the song says, "there is power in the blood."

6. Acknowledge your freedom. Hebrews 10:23 says God wants us to "hold fast the profession of our faith." Hold fast to our "confession." If you battle cigarettes, say "I am free of cigarettes!" If you battle lust or alcohol or drugs, confess that you are no longer a slave to that particular problem.

7. Finally, be filled with God. Ephesians 3:19 says, "Be filled with all fullness of God."

We desperately need to be filled and to stay filled with the Holy Spirit. It is a daily infilling of the Spirit that protects us from the "angry darts" of Satan in the first place. Being filled with the Spirit *is* our shield of faith. A follow-up for deliverance must always include the Spirit-filled life!

4.
He Enables Us

Our first taste of the power of God in our lives is the salvation or conversion experience. That is when our lives are turned around, our hearts are open to the Lord and sensitive to the Holy Spirit, because we have been touched by God. We have just begun to operate in the spiritual realm. The power of God has just become a reality in our lives.

As we begin to experience this power, something happens in our lives. The inner self begins to grow and mature. We begin to change. In fact, change must take place. The power of God is not something that gives us only a "bless-me sensation." The power of God changes us as it pulsates through our beings.

The negative is replaced by the positive. Inner hurts are healed. Bitterness is dissolved. What happens is a blossoming in our spirits as the power of God flows through us.

We derive our sustenance from Christ just as a branch does from the vine. Indeed, Jesus said, "I am the vine; ye are the branches: He that abideth in me, and I in him, the same bringeth forth much fruit: for without me ye can do nothing" (John 15:5).

The Power Of God Produces "Fruits"

That's the point. As we experience God's power, that power in our lives produces something beautiful called fruit — love, joy, peace, long-suffering, gentleness, goodness, faith, meekness, temperance (Gal. 5:22, 23).

Let's not confuse the fruit of the Spirit with the fruits of a Christian. One is always singular in the Bible, the other always plural. Jesus said by their *fruits* ye shall know them.

There are five areas that can only be produced in our lives by the Holy Spirit of God.

1. We must *believe right* (I John 4:1-6). We must believe right about Jesus — that He is very God.

2. We must *love right* (John 13:35). God wants us to love Him, fellow Christians, neighbors and enemies. There is no way we can do this without God's help. That is where the fruit of the Spirit comes in.

3. We must *pray right* (Zech. 4:6). We cannot expect our prayers to be answered every time unless we pray "in the Spirit."

4. We must *live right* (Eph. 4:25-5:5). We deceive no one but ourselves if we think we can be a real Christian without living the life according to Biblical standards. That takes the help of the Spirit of Jesus.

5. We must *produce right* (John 15:16). What comes forth from our lives, whether it be a home, a business, a career, or a church, must have the flow of the power of God or it will eventually come to

naught.

The city where I pastor is known as the World's Citrus Center. There are citrus groves everywhere. Our county produces more oranges than the entire state of California.

I used to live about three blocks from the church. As I walked to church I passed an orange grove. I enjoyed watching the trees blossom each spring and observing the small green fruit appear, grow, and finally turn a luscious orange color in the fall and early winter.

Do you know that I never saw an orange tree agonizing to bear fruit? Nor did I hear those trees groaning and complaining about having to bear fruit. God created them to produce fruit. Given the proper soil, rainfall and climate, that is what they did — produce fruit — year after year.

That is what producing "fruit" in our lives should be like. It should never be hard. It should be an outgrowth of God's power in our lives. As we draw closer to God in prayer and praise, and as we read and meditate on the Word of God, we will produce good fruit as the Spirit of God operates in our lives.

To have an outgrowth of the Spirit of God, we must first have Christ within. When we do, the Bible promises that "God is made unto us wisdom, righteousness, sanctification and redemption" (I Cor. 1:30). This is a wonderful verse that every Christian ought to underline in his Bible.

We have already discussed in Chapter 1 how Christ, who is the power of God, is our redemption (which is, of course, the new birth experience). But what about the others: wisdom, righteousness and sanctification?

The Power Of God Produces Wisdom

First, we have wisdom, which means understanding. The power of God helps us understand things we couldn't understand otherwise. I am not referring to the wisdom which you acquire through the school of hard knocks. You learn, for example, to make the wise business decision from some of the wrong ones you made.

No, the wisdom to which I am referring, is the ability to understand the deeper things of God, so we can see the difference, for example, between what Paul and James each meant when they wrote about faith.

Paul writes in Romans 1:17 that "the just shall live by faith," not works. James writes in James 2:24 that: "ye see then how that by works a man is justified, and not by faith only." A contradiction? Paul says you need faith. James says it is not enough.

Whole denominational trends have been formed over this seeming contradiction in scripture. Some Christians emphasize faith; others, works. But because the power of God gives us wisdom, we can understand that the faith referred to by both Paul and James is actually the Spirit of faith, which is the Holy Spirit.

The works about which Paul writes has to do with the works of the flesh or the works of the law. James, on the other hand, is referring to the good works which come from having faith in the Lord.

Notice what Paul writes in Rom. 1:17: "Therein is

the righteousness of God revealed from faith to faith: as it is written, the just shall life by faith." So the Spirit of God who is the Spirit of righteousness is revealed from generation to generation, from person to person. That Spirit is transferred from individual to individual as others are led to Christ. It produces the works which are necessary to prove that we really have the faith of God. This faith, remember, is the Holy Spirit of God, the gift of God's love.

The Power Of God Produces Sanctification

Finally, we are sanctified, which means to be set apart from the world. Another word for it might be purity. God wants us pure, and this can only come as a work of the Holy Spirit in our lives.

The problem is that many consider sanctification an old-fashioned word or old-fashioned concept. It brings memories of old-fashioned preachers saying you were not sanctified if the women did not wear their hair in a bun or if their sleeves were not wrist length, or if their dress hems were not well below the knees.

Others get side-tracked over sanctification. Many argue whether sanctification occurs all at once like conversion or the infilling of the Holy Spirit, or if it is gradual, like a maturing process.

All I know is that God wants us to be pure — to be set apart from the world. He wants us to lay aside the trappings of the world or anything that would encumber our walk with God.

In the area of sanctification, I believe that one of the finest statements outside the Bible is in the Assemblies of God bylaws:

The Scripture warns against participating in activity which defiles the body, or corrupts the mind and spirit; the inordinate love or preoccupation with pleasures, position or possession, which lead to their misuse; manifestation of extreme behavior, unbecoming speech, or inappropriate appearance; any fascination or association which lessens ones affection for spiritual things (Luke 21:34, 35; Rom. 8:5-8, 12:1, 2; I Cor. 6:14-18; Eph. 5:11; I Tim. 2:8-10; 4:12; James 4:4; I John 2:15-17; Titus 2:12).

By-laws, Article VIII, Sec. 6, page 143
Minutes Revised, 1977

The power of God, then, produces fruit and it produces wisdom, righteousness, sanctification and redemption (I Cor. 1:30). But it does not stop here. The process of producing the fruit of the Spirit is ongoing. It does not happen just once, then quit, any more than a tree bears only one apple, or even one crop of apples, then quits. It happens continually year after year.

When the power of God touches our lives, we are changed and we continue to change as we open ourselves to His Holy Spirit.

But unless we continue, day by day, moment by moment yielding our lives anew and afresh to Jesus Christ, who is the power of God, we are no better off than anyone else. Jesus wants to be on the throne of our lives and each day we ought to give ourselves completely to Him. In fact, we should do it over and over throughout the day.

Paul wrote in II Corinthians 13:4 that we shall "live with Him (Jesus) by the power of God toward you."

In other words, the power of God enables us to live our daily lives. That includes the way we perform on the job, how we do in school, how neat we keep our homes, how we treat family and friends. God wants us to be loving and kind, gentle and patient to people we meet. And He gives us the power through His Holy Spirit to do this.

How can this happen to us? How can we experience the power of God all the time? There is only one way. That is to yield ourselves anew and afresh to God daily through prayer and reading the Word of God.

Read The Word Of God

A number of years ago, before I entered the ministry, I learned first hand the power of reading the Word of God. A friend in college challenged me to read 15 chapters of the Bible a day. He said it would change the expression on my face.

I did not realize I had such a dour looking expression. But I decided I would take the challenge and see if it worked. It almost killed me! It takes about 45 minutes to read 15 chapters, and I didn't have 45 extra minutes in my day.

At the time I was taking a full load of 16 hours at the university. I was delivering papers every morning at 4 a.m., working several hours a day at the radio station. On Saturday afternoon I worked at a clothing store. In addition to that, I performed in the Messiah chorus and a Shakespeare play. My schedule was loaded.

But I disciplined myself to find time to read 15 chapters of the Bible a day. I found I still had time for everything else except goofing off. And my friend was right. Reading the Bible regularly did change the expression on my face!

I challenge you to try it. Read 15 chapters of the Bible every day, and it will brighten the countenance on your face, too.

Praise The Lord

Here is something else to try. Praise God every day, not just once, but seven times. Take time to lift your hands and praise the Lord several times each day. As you do, the Holy Spirit will be drawn to your spirit as to a magnet. The Holy Spirit of God moves in to inhabit the praises of His people.

Then, three times a day, ask God for things. The Bible says, "Evening, and morning and at noon will I pray, and cry aloud: and He shall hear my voice" (Ps. 55:17). If we would praise God seven times a day and make requests three times a day, I believe we will experience God's power in our lives as never before.

I recently experienced a victory in my life when I prayed about a knotty situation. It involved a severed relationship between me and an older friend. I wondered if the relationship would ever be restored.

A young evangelist, Doug Wead, was conducting a meeting in our church. One night he set up a movie screen on the platform. He used it as a prop to get us to picture an answer to prayer.

I visualized the relationship with the man restored.

It seemed an impossible thing. Within days, my friend apologized for wronging me. Our relationship was restored. I was almost as astonished as the group in the book of Acts that was praying for Peter to be released from prison (Acts 12:13-17). When he was released, they could hardly believe it. But prayer changes things!

"Be Ye Being Filled"

My whole point is that we must be conscious every moment of the day of His quickening power and of His enriching presence. I like the way Paul put it in Ephesians 5:18; "And be not drunk with wine, wherein is excess; but be filled (the original says, 'Be ye being filled') with the Spirit." That means "keep on drinking." Keep on drinking of the Holy Spirit of God. Then, he says, "speaking to yourselves in psalms and hymns and spiritual songs, singing and making melody in your heart to the Lord" (Eph. 5:19).

We should continually be singing spiritual songs to ourselves, thinking about Jesus, being filled with His presence. Drink continually of the Spirit of God until you are saturated with His presence. We should always be thanking God for everything. This is how to keep experiencing His power. As we do this, we can experience strength every day. It is a sort of super-human strength given to us by the power of God which is found in the Lord Jesus Christ.

5.
He Keeps Us

We need the power of God in our lives for another very important reason: He keeps us. I'm living proof of His keeping power.

In our own strength we are nothing, but as we depend on the ministry of the Holy Spirit — on the power of God in our lives — God puts a wall of protection around us. Paul said, "I rather glory in my infirmities (in my weaknesses), that the power of Christ may rest upon me" (II Cor. 12:9).

We need that power in our lives every day, whether we are driving the car, mopping the floor, buying the groceries, spanking the children — whatever we do. The power of God keeps us in four areas — from calamity, sickness, sin and death.

He Keeps Us From Calamity

Psalm 91:10 says "there shall no evil befall thee." That is a promise we can claim today. If we are dwelling "in the secret place of the most high," we can expect the Spirit of God to protect us from calamity. God will dispatch angels to watch over us.

MOUNTAIN-MOVING MOTIVATION

And, God will move on the hearts of others to pray for us. I know this is true because it has happened in my own life.

Several years ago my family and I were driving back to Florida after spending Christmas with relatives in Oklahoma. As we drove to Okarche, Oklahoma, it was very cold. It was snowing. Somehow I missed the yield sign, and I pulled into the path of a fully loaded gasoline tanker going 65 miles per hour.

Just as I got onto the highway, I heard the horn blast as loud as a train whistle. I glanced in the rear-view mirror and saw the truck for the first time. He was doing everything he could to stop, but was coming down on me hard; his brakes were screeching and the truck tractor trailer was beginning to hump. It looked as if he might jackknife.

God gave me the presence of mind to swerve quickly to the shoulder of the highway. Just as I did, the truck tore past me in a cloud of snow. The driver was finally able to stop it several hundred feet down the road. Gingerly I pulled behind him and stopped. The driver got down from his big rig. His face was as white as the snow on the highway. He was trembling like a leaf.

He looked at my four little children, my wife, me, and our belongings all piled in the car after Christmas. He shook his head angrily at what almost happened, climbed back in the truck and slowly drove away. Then I realized we had narrowly escaped being killed. I began to tremble too.

When we got home a couple of days later, we

received a call from a lady in our church who has a ministry of intercessory prayer. She and another dear lady who was not even a member of our church had been praying for us. The other sister had had a vision of the yield sign, the gasoline tanker and our car narrowly being missed. At the moment that was happening, these little ladies were praying that God would keep us from calamity and spare our lives. Praise God He did.

A couple of years later, my wife, two daughters and I went boating on the Fourth of July with one of the families of our church. We decided to boat on Lake Eloise in Winter Haven, Florida, not far from where we live. Lake Eloise is the lake next to Cypress Gardens where the famous water ski shows are performed several times a day. Local boaters can get to Lake Eloise through a series of canals and can watch the show from their boats.

As we watched the water ski show a storm began to brew very quickly as it often does in Central Florida that time of year. The advancing storm caused some high waves on the lake. Those waves, added to the wake caused by the water skiers, began to rock our boat. Water began lapping over the side.

We tried to start the motor and move to a less choppy location. But before we could, a large wave hit the boat just as several of us shifted our weight inside the boat. The boat capsized. All seven of us were dumped into 30 feet of murky green water.

I was the first to surface, then our friend Richard, then his wife, Merle, then my wife, Joyce, who was holding Dawn, our youngest daughter in her arms.

But Karla, our other daughter, and Jeffy, our friends' young son, did not come up.

Evidently the children were caught underneath the boat in a little air pocket created when it rolled over. We could hear their pitifully muffled cries coming through the fiberglass. Richard and I dived several times trying to rescue them. But they were trapped. The boat was too heavy to turn over.

Meanwhile, the show must go on. The water skiers continued with their routine while our children were seconds away from suffocation.

Fortunately, two naval reservists were in a nearby boat watching the show from the water as we had been. When they saw we were in trouble, they raced to where we were. I shouted that there were two children underneath the boat. By then their cries had ceased. A terrible sick feeling hit the pit of my stomach. Later, we learned Karla had said to Jeffy, "Shut up, Jeffy. They'll get us out of here!"

The naval reservists couldn't turn the boat over either, but one of them with his hobnail boots ripped loose the canopy from the boat that released the trapped children. Karla, able to swim a little, grabbed Jeffy's hand and said, "Come on, Jeffy. Let's get out of here!" Diving under the boat, the two men grabbed the cooperating children and brought them to the surface. Later, Karla and the two men were decorated for their bravery.

The entire ordeal lasted 20 minutes. While this was happening a little Spirit-filled Presbyterian lady who attends our church was watching television with her husband in Lakeland. She suddenly felt a great burden to pray for the Straders. She excused herself and went to her room at the same time my wife's watch stopped when it hit the water. She prayed for us for 20 minutes, lying on her bed crying out to God for us even though she didn't know why. Then the burden lifted. She knew we were all right.

At the same time, two ladies in our church were walking out of the local general hospital. One looked at the other and said, "I have a strange burden to pray for the Straders." They got in their car, joined hands and prayed for our protection.

We found out later that several days before a little Hungarian lady from my former pastorate in Gary, Indiana, called another lady in the church and told her she felt something dreadful was going to happen to the Straders.

"We've got to warn them," the Hungarian lady said.

"No," said her friend. "Let's just pray that God will protect them."

That's not all. The stories go on.

A few days before the accident, a lady in our church saw a vision of Dawn, our youngest daughter, at the bottom of the lake. Drowned. In her vision, this lady went to Dawn, picked her up and God brought her back to life as she prayed.

The night before the accident, some of the boys in our church went camping at a park right outside Lakeland where we live. Their leader is a big hulk of a man named Ben Stone. In the middle of the night Ben got a burden to pray for me and my family. It was pouring rain, but he draped a sheet around his shoulders and waded into the ankle-deep mud to intercede for our safety.

A couple of the young boys heard Ben praying and they stuck their heads out of the tent. They saw this giant of a man draped in a sheet and silhouetted against the lights of the city. They didn't know what to think. They dived back into their sleeping bags, scared to death.

Then, the morning of the accident, a group of ladies met for a prayer meeting, even though it was the Fourth of July. One of them said they had a burden to pray for the Richard Jones' family — the family in the boat with us. Someone else spoke up that they had a burden to pray for the Straders. No one knew our two families were to be together that day. They prayed for our safety.

Then, our associate pastor felt an urge to pray specifically for Karla, our oldest daughter, who was trapped under the boat in a pocket of air. He saw her shrouded in blackness and he prayed for her safety.

As incredible as these stories are, they are all true. I believe God moved on these people's hearts to intercede for us. He answered their prayers, and kept us from calamity!

If we will dwell in the secret place of the most High, God's Spirit leads us to pray and God's Spirit helps us even when danger is all around us. I praise God for the protecting power of the Lord Jesus Christ.

God Keeps Us From Sickness

God keeps us not only from calamity, but from

sickness. He promises us in Psalm 91:10 that "neither shall any plague come nigh thy dwelling." If we live as we ought to live, we can avoid much sickness because of the Spirit of God.

I know what pain and sickness are. Before I came to Christ, I was weak, sickly and skinny. But when I gave my life totally to Jesus at age 16, all that changed. My health began to improve. The grace of God began to be evidenced in my soul through the Spirit of God. Particularly since I have been Baptized in the Holy Spirit, I have known nothing but good health. I praise God for health that only He can give.

I believe sickness results from basically two things. Either we have sinned, or God is allowing us to be tested.

God allowed Job to be tested. Most of us remember the story about Job. The Bible records that he was a "man perfect and upright" (Job 1:1). He went through a severe test in which he lost all his possessions and children and was covered from head to toe with boils because God gave Satan permission to attack him. God wanted to see what kind of man Job really was. Job came through the test with flying colors. God restored twice everything Job lost.

Sometimes God wants to see what we are made of. He allows us to be tested. I should add here that some of us go through more tests than we need to because we refuse to test or examine ourselves. I Corinthians 11:31 says if we judge (test) ourselves, we wouldn't have to be judged.

When we go through a test of sickness (and all of

us are subject to this in the sovereign will of God) God can bring us out of that sickness in complete deliverance. But we must learn our lesson and believe God to heal us.

I am dismayed when I visit the hospital and see some of our fine Christian people watching television at the foot of their beds. Or, they read magazines or worldly novels. That is exactly what they *don't* need. They should be reading the Word of God.

When we are sick, we need to saturate ourselves with the Word of God. We need large doses of the Word even more than medicine when we're sick. Yet on occasion Christians allow their minds to be clouded with the things of the world rather than seeking God for their healing.

If we will read God's Word, meditate on God's Word and pray, believing God's Word, we will give God a much greater opportunity to let His healing virtue flow. Actually, we would come closer to staying out of the hospital all together if we would stay in the Word of God when we are well. But sometimes the Lord has to allow us "to lie down" before we'll take time for Him.

God wants us to take out that time on a regular basis — not just when we are sick. As we get the Word of God inside us, and as it becomes alive inside us, then it gives us an immunity. This doesn't mean that we will never be sick, but we will certainly be a lot healthier if we yield ourselves daily to the Holy Spirit of God and to His Word.

He Keeps Us From Sin

Jesus said in Matthew 5:48, "Be ye therefore perfect, even as your Father which is in heaven is per-fect." I John 3:9 says, "Whosoever is born of God doth not commit sin; for his seed remaineth in him: and he cannot sin, because he is born of God."

The Bible gives us an impossible command — "Be perfect!" Yet none of us are totally without sin. We are human, and it is part of our human nature to sin. There is no way to live above sin in our own strength. So why then, does God command that we be perfect? Because He wants to "aim" for the goal of perfection. His keeping power is available to keep us from sin.

The Spirit of the living God can help keep our thought life pure; keep our words clean; keep our actions above reproach. When we are born into the family of God, we become kings and priests. Royal blood flows through our veins. As members of the family of God, we are to live above sin. And, God gives us the power to do this.

Because of our access to this power to keep us from sin, there is no excuse for any Christian to sin. The Bible says, "Whosoever ... is begotten of God keepeth himself and that wicked one toucheth him not" (I John 5:18). I believe that a Christian who is truly walking with God doesn't have to make mistakes. Doesn't the scripture say, "Do not err my beloved brethren" (James 1:16)?

God can keep us from sin in the perfect will of God. If you and I will be perfectly yielded to the Holy Spirit we can live above sin. No evil thought or word or deed in our lives ever needs to displease God as we live and move and have our being in Him.

He Keeps Us From Eternal Death

I believe in eternal security. Now before you jump to any conclusions about my doctrine let me hasten to explain. I believe we are eternally secure as long as we stay in the hollow of God's hand. Look at John 10:28: "And I give unto them eternal life; and they shall never perish, neither shall any man *pluck* them out of my father's hand."

The key phrase here is "neither shall any man pluck them out of my father's hand." No power on heaven or earth can remove us from God's family. We are eternally secure while we stay in the hollow of his hand.

But we have free wills. This is where the kicker comes in. We can resign from God's family any time we want to. If we become disappointed with the program, we can get out. I promise you that if we depart from God, He will part from us (II Chron. 15:2). However, He will never leave us or forsake us as long as we don't leave Him or forsake Him.

James 1:14, 15 says: "But every man is tempted, when he is drawn away of his own lust and enticed. Then, when lust hath conceived, it bringeth forth sin: and sin, when it is finished bringeth forth death."

Imagine for a minute that the Christian walk could be illustrated on the blackboard with a straight line drawn on a graph showing progress upwards. God wants our walk with Him to be continually upward, along the "straight and narrow," as the Bible calls it. But, as a rule, most of us, though we show progress have a somewhat uneven course, mostly up, but not always.

But imagine that I draw the line upward a little way, then show a downward line toward the bottom of the blackboard. This illustrates someone who begins to walk with God, but is enticed away with lust or runaway desires. We don't backslide overnight, but as sinful desires overtake our lives, we continue along that downward line until we reach the bottom of the blackboard which would represent spiritual death.

God is not a "bully" sitting on a throne in heaven waiting for us to sin so he can damn us to hell. He is our Father. He loves us and wants us to live moral lives and to be full of the Holy Spirit.

But if we let sin get into our lives, it keeps us from going onward and upward with God. It begins a trend that will ultimately result in spiritual death. That is, unless we turn our lives over to the Lord again.

We are born again only once when we come into God's family, but we can be saved many times. If we deviate from that straight and narrow path of following Jesus, we must come back to the main-line — to "the secret place of the most High" and hide our lives once again in God.

Psalm 91:1 says, "He that dwelleth in the secret place of the most High shall abide under the shadow of the Almighty." You and I don't have to deviate from the very direct center of God's will. When we are there, God gives us protection by His angels. He gives us protection by His Holy Spirit.

We need to strive for the center of God's will. Unfortunately, many people deviate from God's will, even though they are still headed in the same basic direction. It's as if they are on a parallel line, just a few inches below the chalk line I described above. They are going to heaven, but they aren't in the *center* of God's perfect will.

They are in what I call God's *permissive will.* Often this creates many struggles and problems for them. We should allow God to help us, by His Spirit, to find the center of His perfect will so we could avoid the problems and attacks from Satan for which this leaves us open.

I like to think of being in God's will as being in a sort of a cocoon of God's blessing. It's like having a shield of faith around us. What is that shield of faith? It is the Spirit of the Living God.

Recently one of my associates was dealing with a man who wandered into our church off the streets. The man had been into Satan worship and was possessed with evil spirits. As my associate ministered deliverance to this man, the man lunged at him with the strength of 10 men.

The associate had reason to be frightened because the man was a large man with a great deal of natural strength. But just inches before the man pounced on my associate, he stopped. It was as if God stopped him dead in his tracks. The man couldn't touch him. There seemed to be a wall of protection around my young associate. The man was stopped by the power of God.

The young associate continued to minister deliverance until the man completely calmed down and was totally delivered by the power of God. He left the church that day full of peace and joy and blessing because of the power of God.

We need this wall of protection that the Holy Spirit provides. In our own strength we are weak; we are nothing. We must depend on the ministry of the power of God in our lives. The Apostle Paul wrote: "most gladly therefore will I rather glory in my infirmities (or in my weaknesses), that the power of Christ may rest upon me" (II Cor. 12:9). Whatever we are doing, we need God to help us yield ourselves continually to the Spirit of the power of God so we will have this protection.

6.
He Motivates Us

When Jesus was crucified, His disciples were so frightened they all fled, except for John. Even after Jesus' resurrection when He spent 40 days with them, they were still frightened. They had no power. They lacked motivation.

Just before Jesus ascended into heaven, He promised His disciples to send them a Comforter to be with them. Then, He told them to go back to Jerusalem to tarry. He told them in Acts 1:8 "But ye shall receive power, after that the Holy Ghost is come upon you: and ye shall be witnesses unto me both in Jerusalem, and in all Judea, and in Samaria, and unto the uttermost part of the earth."

They went back to Jerusalem, and just as Jesus said, the Holy Spirit descended on them 10 days later — on the Jewish feast of Pentecost. They were "filled with the Holy Ghost and began to speak with other tongues, as the Spirit gave them utterance" (Acts 2:4).

That was the birthday of the church.

MOUNTAIN-MOVING MOTIVATION

The 120 who were gathered in the upper room that day made so much noise as they worshipped God that people from all over Jerusalem gathered to find out what was going on. There was so much commotion that some said they were drunk. Peter stood up and told the crowd they were only seeing the fulfillment of Joel's prophecy, that in the last days God would pour out His Spirit upon all flesh.

Then Peter began to tell the crowd about Jesus. When he was through, 3,000 people "received his word and were baptized" (Acts 2:41). A few days later 5,000 more converts were added. Something startling happened that day in the upper room that took 120 frightened, confused people and motivated them to take the world for Jesus.

That was the initial outpouring of the Holy Spirit. In our own century the Holy Spirit has been out-poured in a special way. Many who received the Baptism in the Holy Spirit in the early part of the 20th Century called themselves "pentecostals" after the Day of Pentecost when the 120 first received the Baptism in the Holy Spirit as recorded in Acts 2.

My introduction to pentecostals was Oral Roberts. My parents took me to one of his tent meetings in Oklahoma City, Oklahoma, in the mid-1940s. I had never seen anything like it in my life. There were 10,000 people packed in that stiffling hot tent listening to him preach and watching the miracles.

I had never seen a miracle before. But that night I saw people come out of wheel chairs and off stretch-ers. I saw Brother Roberts cast evil spirits out of people. I also heard for the first time people speak in "other tongues." I was so challenged by what I saw that I determined I wanted to be like Oral Roberts.

I remember Brother Roberts commented that night that the preachers who were sitting on the platform "believe like I do." When they were introduced I noticed that each one belonged to a pentecostal denomination like the Assemblies of God, the Pentecostal Holiness or the Church of the Four Square Gospel. If I wanted to be like Oral Roberts, I reasoned, then I needed to become a pentecostal.

That was my first motivation to seek the Baptism in the Holy Spirit. But unlike the Apostles who tarried in Jerusalem for only 10 days before they received the Holy Spirit, I tarried nine long years.

During those nine years a lot of well-meaning pentecostal folk tried to help me receive the Baptism. Some gave me strange formulas for receiving, and usually I did whatever they told me to do.

People told me to raise one hand, then the other, then both hands at once. Some told me to "hold on." Others said to "let go." I tried lying flat on my back and flat on my face.

Some people pounded me on the back as I prayed. I even had a few get "ahold of my golly-hopper," as we would have said out in Western Oklahoma, and wiggle it back and forth. Some told me to say "glory, glory, glory" real fast. You name it, I tried it — all in an attempt to receive the Baptism in the Holy Spirit.

The Holy Spirit has been poured out on many people in denominational churches in the past decade. This has generally been called the charismatic renewal. There have been teachers in the charismatic renewal who say you don't have to tarry to receive the Baptism in the Holy Spirit. Some teach on receiving the Baptism in the Holy Spirit, then tell everyone in the audience that they should just receive it. Right then. With no tarrying.

You know what? Thousands of people have received the Baptism in the Holy Spirit this way. These people are just open to the Lord. Because they are open, they receive. They don't know receiving the Baptism in the Holy Spirit is supposed to be hard, or that you have to "tarry" nine years like I did.

Some "old-line pentecostals" think this method is "zipping them through" too fast. "People should tarry for the Holy Spirit," they say. Well, I wasn't "zipped through" too fast. I would prefer the "zipped through" method any day.

When I was 25 years old, I had already sought the Baptism in the Holy Spirit for several years. I had just graduated from seminary, had gotten married, and had the call of God on my life to preach the Gospel. But I had cold feet about preaching. I knew I needed the Baptism in the Spirit before I could preach with anointing.

In the fall of that year, I really got serious with God. The scripture says, "the violent take it by force" (Matt. 11:12). I purposed in my heart that I was going to receive the Baptism in the Holy Spirit. But even with my new determination, it wasn't easy.

For example, one night I was seeking God at the altar after a service in a pentecostal church. The Spirit was moving and I was receiving a blessing. I thought I might receive the Baptism that night. But two dear old pentecostal ladies were standing behind me talking about their chickens. I finally gave up seeking the Lord, rather than listen to their silly conversation while I tried to keep my thoughts on the Lord.

The next morning I was still determined to pray so I went down to First Assembly in Greenville, South Carolina, and asked the janitor for a key. I found a Sunday school room in the basement where I could pray in privacy. I paced back and forth and read the scriptures as I walked. I knew the Bible says "faith cometh by hearing, and hearing by the Word of God" (Romans 10:17), so I read the Bible out loud awhile to increase my faith. Then I prayed.

I had eaten no breakfast, but when noon came I kept praying. I was not hungry. I prayed all afternoon. About 5 p.m. the janitor came around to see how I was doing. He was a skinny pimply-faced teenager — probably not out of junior high. He wanted to know if I would like him to help me pray for the Baptism in the Holy Spirit.

God certainly knew how to crucify my pride. There I was, at least 10 years older than he, a graduate of a seminary and probably a lot more spiritual than he. And he was going to help *me* pray. I said it was okay, not expecting much to happen.

In a few minutes, however, the power of God came down on that boy. His tongue was going a mile a minute. He was speaking in other tongues as the Spirit gave him utterance. I couldn't believe it. It was I who was seeking the Baptism, and now God was baptizing him all over in the Holy Spirit. It didn't seem fair. After awhile, he finished praying and left. I prayed alone for a few more hours until Dick — a nephew on my wife's side — came by the church. He saw the light on and stuck his head in the door to find out what was going on.

My nephew was a nice boy. He was a member of that particular church and had already received the Baptism in the Holy Spirit. He wore his long blond hair in a dove-tail haircut that was popular back in 1954. Even though he loved the Lord, I knew he couldn't hold a candle to my consecration. I witnessed to someone about the Lord every day. Dick probably didn't witness once a week. I read 15 chapters of the Bible every day. Dick did well to read a chapter a day. I spent an hour a day in prayer. I knew Dick probably didn't pray more than 15 minutes a day.

He wanted to know if he could pray with me. I said okay. Soon his hands were extended like two lightning rods. He was experiencing the power of God in a beautiful way. Suddenly he was magnifying God in a language that he had never learned. Then, the power of God hit that boy so hard that he fell back on the floor of that Sunday school classroom.

Dick was the first "holy-roller" I had ever seen. He rolled to the right then to the left. All this time he was praising God in other tongues. All this discouraged me because I was wanting to receive the Baptism in the Holy Spirit. Everyone was receiving it but me.

What I learned later was that God is no respecter of persons. God does not care what we try to do to *deserve* the Holy Spirit. He does not decide to pour out His Spirit on us based on our consecration. The Holy Spirit is a gift of God that I merely had to receive.

I also began to see that I was so prejudiced toward pentecostals in my earlier years that God was letting me go through this wilderness experience of seeking for the Baptism in the Holy Spirit long enough to get those prejudices out of my system.

Finally later that night, my wife and mother-in-law came by the church and talked me into coming home and going to bed. But I was back at the church early the next day. I read more of the Word and prayed. After a few hours, however, I felt as though I was at the end of my rope.

I called the pastor of the church — George Gould, a precious man of God in whom I had a great deal of respect. I asked him to pray with me for the Baptism in the Holy Spirit. He knelt next to me at one of the wooden chairs in that little Sunday school room and we began to quietly worship the Lord.

The atmosphere was charged with the Holy Spirit. I sensed a strange stirring. A sensation began to rise in my heart like an artesian well. It bubbled up like a fountain until the pressure reached my throat. My tongue became a bit thick and my lips got dry. I noticed that praising God in English was becoming difficult. Then all of a sudden a strange syllable came out of the corner of my mouth. Could this be the Baptism in the Holy Spirit? But I had expected this to be an overwhelmingly emotional experience. I thought I'd be rolling around on the floor now like Dick had done the evening before.

Suddenly I uttered a foreign-sounding word, then a phrase. Finally I said a whole sentence in a language I had never learned. Then, the whole top blew off, as they would say in oil country. I really hit a gusher. The power of God welled up within my heart. I had expected something to fall from heaven, but I was being filled with the streams of living water that Jesus said would well up from within.

I praised God in that foreign language for an hour and a half. Pastor Gould called my wife and mother-in-law. They came to the church and rejoiced with me that after seeking God for nine years I finally received the Baptism in the Holy Spirit!

Receiving the Baptism in the Holy Spirit totally revolutionized my life and ministry. I was a young preacher right out of seminary, but I lacked anointing when I preached. It was amazing what happened in such a short time.

The same night Pastor Gould asked me to speak at First Assembly. I spoke with power and authority. The change in me must have been a little like the change in Peter. Less than two months before his Day of Pentecost sermon where 3,000 were saved, he had denied Christ three times. The difference in his ministry — and in mine — was the Baptism in the Holy Spirit.

A few weeks later I preached my first revival in Indiana. It lasted three weeks. People were healed, saved and blessed.

The blessing the day I received the Baptism in the Holy Spirit was wonderful. But it doesn't compare to the blessing since then. I have pastored two churches in Indiana, served as dean of men of a Bible college, and denominational state youth director. Since I began pastoring my present congregation more than 12 years ago, the attendance has increased from 325 to more than 3,000.

The worldwide ministry of the church includes a school, radio and tv ministry, book and cassette ministry and a church magazine. To God be the glory.

One of the most beautiful things about the Holy Spirit is that He motivates us. Having the power of the Holy Spirit is much, much more than merely experiencing the Baptism in the Holy Spirit as I have just described. He motivates us to exercise the gifts of the Spirit and also to witness to others.

Gifts of the Spirit

The gifts of the Spirit are listed in I Corinthians 12:7-10: "But the manifestation of the Spirit is given to every man to profit withal. For to one is given by the Spirit the word of wisdom; to another the word of knowledge by the same Spirit; to another faith by the same Spirit; to another the gifts of healing by the same Spirit; to another the working of miracles; to another prophecy; to another discerning of spirits; to another divers kinds of tongues; to another the interpretation of tongues." Then the scripture says: "But all these worketh that one and the selfsame Spirit, dividing to every man severally as He will." Let's examine these gifts of the Spirit one by one.

MOUNTAIN-MOVING MOTIVATION

The Word of Wisdom

This is a beautiful gift of God, and perhaps one of the greatest. It is frequently manifested in the middle of a sermon, a counseling session or even a business meeting. It is always the right word at the right time for a specific need.

For example, the word of wisdom was in operation when an evangelist and I visited a man in our church named Les who had been healed in the revival meetings. He had been a railroad engineer, but had severely injured his back and was laid off by the railroad.

God had miraculously healed his back. He was able to take off the back brace he had been wearing. We knew he had gone to the company doctor to confirm the healing. Then, he stopped coming to church. The evangelist and I went by his home to see what was wrong.

Even though Les was healed, did not need to wear a back brace, and had no pain whatsoever, the X-rays taken by the company doctor showed a small bone was still missing. The doctor was afraid his back condition might worsen and recommended the railroad not rehire him.

My friend was totally demoralized. He could not understand why God had not put a new bone into place when He healed him. Then the Lord gave a word of wisdom to the evangelist who was with me.

"Les," he said, "God evidently does not want you back on the railroad. He has something better for you. Now, isn't it even a greater miracle that you're well and strong even with that small bone still missing in your back?"

Les jumped up from his chair. "So it is! So it is!" He was so moved by that word of wisdom that he began to laugh and cry at the same time. That had been a beautiful word of wisdom just for him at the time he needed it.

Word of Knowledge

This gift operates when the Holy Spirit lets us know something that it would be impossible to know otherwise. This is the gift Kathryn Kuhlman used when she called out during a Miracle Service that someone in the balcony, for example, had just been healed of deafness in the left ear. Then that person would discover that he had indeed just been healed.

This gift has also operated in my own ministry. One night during a camp meeting I was preaching in Canada, God showed me during the altar service that an older man and his wife were at the meeting who had never really been born again, even though they had attended church and been "religious" all their lives. All their friends, their children and grand-children thought they were saved, but they weren't.

I shared publicly what God had shown me. Sure enough, there was a couple in the audience who fit that description. The couple took that manifestation as a sign God was calling them to make peace with Him. They came forward and confirmed that the word of knowledge was true. Then they knelt at the altar, surrendered their lives to God and were truly born again.

Faith

Faith is one of the greatest gifts. I believe that a

pastor who builds a church building, a radio station, or a new school must be operating in faith, or the project will fail.

The gift of faith was operating at my church one time when I challenged our people to help provide scholarships so needy children could attend our Christian school. At the time we were in a building program for a much needed new gymnasium, and we really needed the money I asked them to give for scholarships to go to the building program instead.

We proceeded in faith, however, and the people gave generously toward the scholarships. At the same time, God provided money so that within a few months' time we were able to complete the new gymnasium completely free of debt.

Gifts of Healing

The Bible promises healing to all believers when they meet God's conditions. The gifts of healing are different. They are manifested whether the person meets the conditions or not.

Along with the other sign gifts, these operate in the sovereign will of God. When faith is high and the Holy Spirit is flowing, the gifts operate according to the will of God. The gifts of healing, for example, were operating at Kathryn Kuhlman's Miracle Services and at the tent revivals of Oral Roberts which I mentioned earlier. Because the gifts operate according to the will of God, sometimes people who are not even believers are healed. It was nothing they did to deserve the healing, but rather the gift of healing in operation.

Working of Miracles

I like Oral Roberts' expression, "Expect A Miracle." Every Christian should live continually expecting miracles, even though the Bible does not promise us one every time we ask.

When a healing is instantaneous, it is a miracle. Miracles have to do with defying the laws of nature — things like turning water into wine, walking on the water, raising the dead.

As a rule, healing comes rather gradually when someone is prayed for. Jesus said, "They shall lay hands on the sick, and they shall recover" (Mark 16:18). Remember the nobleman in the scripture whose son was healed asked his servants when he had begun "to mend" (John 4:52).

Practically all the healings performed by the Lord were miraculous. The gift of the working of miracles was utilized by the Holy Spirit flowing through Him. Also, the gift of the working of miracles is exercised when evil spirits are cast out (Mark 9:39).

At one time in my ministry I had been fighting a terrible hoarseness for more than three months. There were nodules on my vocal chords. The doctor said they would have to be surgically removed. I was preaching at a summer camp in North Carolina when suddenly my voice cleared up.

Later I learned that an "old-timer" in my church had been interceding for my voice to be healed!

Prophecy

Paul says prophecy is one of the greatest gifts. It may be "fore-telling" or "forth-telling." It is always for edification, exhortation and comfort.

After I received the Baptism in the Holy Spirit, I remember how I longed for the gift of prophecy even though several of the other gifts were operating in my life.

Now, when the gift is exercised in my life, it is as if I am reading the words of God line by line off an unfolding scroll in the sky.

Personal prophecies should be judged carefully as well as prophecies for a congregation. Everything should be confirmed by the witness of the Spirit in other believers and checked by the Word of God.

There is a reason for this. The voice of God and the voice of Satan are so very close that it sometimes takes discernment of several persons to distinguish between the two. Satan attempts to mimic God. If we do not "watch and pray" we can be deceived. That is one of the reasons we need the rest of the Body of Christ and must not isolate ourselves. Persons who are isolated are more apt to be deceived. Solomon wisely wrote: "In the multitude of counselors there is safety" (Prov. 11:14).

Discerning of Spirits

Often you hear people talk about the "gift of discernment." This is not one of the gifts of the Spirit. People who claim this "gift" frequently have only the "gift of suspicion," as my friend Roy Harthern says.

The scriptural gift is the "gift of discerning of spirits," not the "gift of discernment." It is given so that we can detect evil spirits, then cast them out in the name of Jesus.

In the Book of Acts, Paul perceived that a young

woman who was disturbing his meetings had evil spirits. Some might have thought she was merely retarded or mentally unbalanced. Paul saw, however, through the gift of discerning of spirits that her problem was deeper than that. He saw what her real problem was.

He turned to her and said, "I command thee in the name of Jesus Christ to come out of her!" (Acts 16:18). She was delivered.

Many times sickness is caused by evil spirits. We know that all sickness is actually caused by the enemy. But many specific sicknesses are caused by specific evil spirits. In the ministry of Jesus, there were many times in which he cast out the spirit of infirmity (Luke 13:11), or a "dumb and deaf spirit" (Mark 9:25).

I have discovered when I pray for the sick that there are evil spirits involved which need to be cast out in about half the cases. This is according to scripture, because about half the recorded incidents of healing in the life of Jesus had to do with evil spirits. We must identify these evil spirits so we can cast them out in the name of Jesus!

Tongues

There are two types of speaking in tongues which are easily and frequently confused. One is a result of our being baptized in the Holy Spirit. This is what happened on the Day of Pentecost when the 120 were in the upper room and "spake with other tongues as the Spirit gave them utterance" (Acts 2:4).

Many call this a "prayer language." That is a beautiful description because we use the tongues in our own private prayer to speak to God. Hardly a day has passed in the past 25 years that I haven't prayed in tongues in my private devotions.

It is a beautiful way to let our spirits communicate directly with God in a way that edifies ourselves. The Bible says, "beloved, (build) up yourselves on your most holy faith, praying in the Holy Ghost" (Jude 20).

Paul wrote to the Corinthian church, "I would that ye all spake with tongues" (I Cor. 14:5).

There is a second type of speaking in tongues that is a gift of the Holy Spirit. Unlike the prayer language for private use which we can use any time or any place, this gift is for public use, and we must wait for the prompting of the Holy Spirit.

If you have attended a pentecostal or charismatic service, you have probably seen someone rise during the meeting and speak for one to three minutes in a language you did not understand. Then either the same person would give a one to three minute exhortation in English or someone else would do it. What you saw in operation was the "gift of tongues" and its twin the "gift of interpretation of tongues."

Frequently tongues are given in a "heavenly language" which no one understands. But often the tongues are actual human languages. The foreign guests in Jerusalem on the Day of Pentecost each heard their own language spoken by those who were praying in tongues in the upper room. Missionaries have come home with stories of having heard people on the mission field who had never studied English pray in fluent English. Entire books have been written to document this phenomenon.

Once I gave a message in tongues at a Sunday morning service in South Bend, Indiana. A lady came to me after the service and said I spoke in fluent Spanish.

Interpretation of Tongues

This gift must go hand in hand with the gift of tongues. Paul says interpretation is necessary. "If there be no interpreter, let him (the one who speaks in tongues during the public service) keep silence in the church," Paul writes in I Corinthians 14:28.

Interpretation of tongues is very similar to prophecy in that God is speaking to His people through a spokesman's lips. The difference is that it comes after a message in tongues. The interpretation is just that — an interpretation, thought-for-thought of the message in tongues. It is not a word-for-word translation.

Evidence

Although speaking in tongues as mentioned in Acts 2:4 is cited by most classical pentecostals as being the *initial* physical, scriptural evidence for receiving the Baptism in the Holy Spirit, (and I believe that is true), the scripture makes it clear that *witnessing* is one of the *main* evidences.

"But ye shall receive power, after that the Holy Ghost is come upon you: and ye shall be witnesses unto me both in Jerusalem, and in all Judea, and in Samaria, and unto the uttermost part of the earth" (Acts 1:8).

When a person is filled with the Spirit, and stays filled with the Spirit, he wants to witness. Evangelism becomes a part of his personality.

It is interesting that there is one Baptism in the Holy Spirit, but there are many fillings. We must continually remain filled. The same group that was filled with the Holy Spirit in Acts 2 was filled *again* with the Holy Spirit in Acts 4. This time it does not say they spoke with other tongues. Rather, they "spake the word of God with boldness" (Acts 4:31).

The Baptism in the Holy Spirit is the door to a new dimension of the Christian experience.

I challenge every Christian to receive this exciting experience of the power of God!

How to Receive the Baptism in the Holy Spirit

Part of the reason it took me nine years to receive the Baptism in the Holy Spirit was that I never received adequate instructions. Some of my pentecostal friends told me to "praise God." Others said to "yield." Both are necessary. But they never told me the third part: "respond to God."

Here is a formula I believe will help you receive the motivating power of God in the Baptism in the Holy Spirit.

1. Praise God

Praise is the way we approach God. The Psalmist says to "enter into his gates with thanksgiving, and into his courts with praise" (Ps. 100:4). When we praise God, we are complimenting Him. We are telling Him we appreciate who He is and what He has done for us. We thank Him for so great a salvation and for keeping His hand on our lives.

We also praise God for the fact He is God. We praise His name because it is holy and greatly to be praised. We should also praise Him in advance for receiving the Baptism in the Holy Spirit.

2. Yield to God

Yielding to God goes beyond praise. It means that we worship Him. Praise and worship are different. Praise is thanking God, complimenting God. Worship means we surrender ourselves fully to God. Every fiber, every blood vessel, every part of our bodies as well as all our entire spirit and soul to God.

As we yield to God, we sell out all our own ambitions, hopes, dreams and aspirations. We hold back nothing. Our will, our spirit, the inner core of our being is surrendered completely to God in unconditional commitment. As we worship with this intensity, coupled with praise, God's Holy Spirit is drawn to us like a magnet. At this point we respond.

3. Respond to God

The scripture says, they "began to speak with other tongues, as the Spirit gave them utterance" (Acts 2:4). Another way to say that is that the Spirit *prompted* them. *They* did the speaking.

When we receive the Baptism in the Holy Spirit, the Spirit merely prompts us to speak. It is our vocal chords; our voice; our lips.

It is like standing on stage in a Christmas play and forgetting our lines. A prompter is off stage ready to whisper the lines just loud enough for us to hear what to say next. That is what the Holy Spirit does. He is a prompter.

I like the way Isaiah put it."Thine ears shall hear a word behind thee, saying, This is the way, walk ye in it" (Isa. 30:21). You might ask how we know it is the voice of God, not the voice of Satan. The way we know is that the inner prompting from the Holy Spirit tells us to praise God and to worship Him. Satan never tells us to do that. The voice of Satan discourages, depresses, condemns. But the voice of God is full of praise and joy and peace.

Remember one more thing. If we ask God for the Baptism in the Holy Spirit, He has promised to give it to us. Jesus said if an earthly father would not give his children stones or serpents instead of food when they ask, how much more will our heavenly Father give us good things when we pray (Matt. 7:9-11).

I challenge you now to begin praising God, to yield to God and to respond to God. You, too, will experience the motivating power of the Holy Spirit.

7.
He Quickens Us

The Holy Spirit makes us alive. The power of God is our energy. The power of God should be flowing through our lives consistently every day as a daily experience with God.

The Bible says, "And God hath both raised up the Lord, and will also raise up us by His own power" (I Cor. 6:14). The Holy Spirit of God will quicken us at the resurrection. But the Holy Spirit is also quickening us right now! The word quicken means to make alive. When the Bible talks about the quick and the dead, it means those who are living and those who have died.

This wonderful Holy Spirit, the Spirit of Christ, which is the power of God that is given to us, is the energy that keeps us moving out in God and growing in the Lord every day.

He Quickens Us in This Life

Romans 8:11 says, "But if the Spirit of Him that raised up Jesus from the dead dwell in you, He that raised up Christ from the dead shall also quicken your mortal bodies by His Spirit that dwelleth in you." This indicates that we are going to be quickened at the resurrection but it indicates that we are also quickened right now by the Holy Spirit in *this present life*.

There are many ways that God quickens us by His power if we let Him. Here are 12 of the most important.

Pray Without Ceasing

Prayer is communication with God. I Thessalonians 5:17 tells us to pray without ceasing. In other words, we should be so tuned in our spirits to the Spirit of God that we are in constant communication. We can be solving problems on the job, or typing a letter, or spanking the children and praying at the same time.

Prayer does not have to be conscious. We don't have to form the words to our prayers in our mind or speak them with our mouths. We can allow our spirits to pray continually. But how? The only way is through the quickening power of the Holy Spirit. As the Spirit quickens our spirits, the Spirit prays through us. The deepest desires of our souls are communicated in this way to the Father.

The Bible tells us that the Spirit prays for us when we don't know how to pray. "The Spirit itself maketh intercession for us with groanings which cannot be uttered. And He that searcheth the hearts knoweth what is the mind of the Spirit, because He maketh intercession for the saints according to the will of God" (Rom. 8:26, 27). Isn't that beautiful? This scripture promises that we pray in the will of God when we pray in the Spirit.

There are many ways we can pray. We can pray in English or in tongues. We can pray silently or out loud. The important thing is that our prayers are quickened by the Holy Spirit. Otherwise, they will merely bounce off the ceiling.

Another scripture says, "Beloved, building up yourselves on your most holy faith, praying in the Holy Ghost" (Jude 20). This is the way to get prayers answered — praying in the Holy Spirit whether it is English, in another tongue, groanings that cannot be uttered, or just a sincere desire going up from our spirits to God's Spirit. We should be conscious of that and believe God for that every moment of the day.

Dwell Richly in God's Word

Colossians 3:16 says, "Let the Word of Christ dwell in you richly in all wisdom; teaching and admonishing one another in psalms and hymns and spiritual songs, singing with grace in your hearts to the Lord."

Anyone who tries to read and understand the Bible without the Holy Spirit quickening his mind is going to come away with some weird interpretations. No one can know what the Bible is saying unless the Spirit of God helps him understand it. The Bible without the activating power of the Holy Spirit will kill and damn and destroy. The Bible itself says, "The letter killeth, but the Spirit giveth life" (II Cor. 3:6).

Every time you and I read the scriptures we should respond to the Holy Spirit and yield ourselves so that

He can flow through us and help us understand what we are reading.

Our brains are not saved yet. We are "waiting for the adoption, to wit, the redemption of our body," but the Spirit within us can activate our brains and quicken them so we can understand what God is saying through His Word.

The wisdom of this world is foolishness with God. The logic of men is not going to give us the right answer with spiritual things. We must have that quickening of the Spirit of God, or we are not going to be able to understand God's Word.

God speaks to us in many ways. There is prophecy, interpretation of tongues, and the still small voice we hear in our spirits. God also speaks to us through nature, or sometimes through accident or tragedy. But God speaks to us through His Word! The Bible not only contains God's Word, it *is* God's Word. However, we are going to miss what God is saying in His Word unless it is quickened to our spirits by the Holy Spirit.

Rejoice Continually

The scripture says, "Rejoice in the Lord alway: and again I say, Rejoice" (Phil. 4:4). How can we rejoice without the Spirit of God quickening us? We can't. Our bodies, our souls, our spirits will be channels through which the Holy Spirit can flow.

There must be a communication line to heaven that contacts the throne of God so that the Spirit of God is consistently flowing through our lives and then given back to God in worship. Our spirits must be blended with God's Spirit. This is a very real experience. It is something you can feel, not always in your body not even always in your soul, but *in your spirit*. You *know* that you *know* that you *know* that it is real.

As the Holy Spirit quickens us, we can sense God's presence continually. This is what gives us joy. Notice I didn't say happiness. God doesn't promise that we will be happy all the time. But He does promise that we will be full of joy continually. Out of this joy, our happiness comes. This is why we can rejoice always, even if circumstances don't look good. We can rejoice even when we are walking through the valley, because our spirits are on the mountaintop. We can have a song even in the middle of the night because of the joy of the Lord.

God gives us no promise of an abundant victorious life here without the flow of the Spirit. God gives absolutely no promise of eternal life without the witness of the Spirit. But if we have it, then we know we have an abundant life here and a victorious entrance into heaven.

Fight Constantly

1 Timothy 6:12 says, "Fight the good fight of faith, lay hold on eternal life, whereunto thou art also called, and hast professed a good profession before many witnesses."

As I have said in earlier chapters, our fight is not against flesh and blood. It is against the devil. The scripture says in Ephesians 6:12 that "We wrestle not against flesh and blood, but against ... spiritual wickedness in high places." The spiritual wickedness, of course, is the kingdom of Satan.

MOUNTAIN-MOVING MOTIVATION

You will remember that the seven sons of Sceva used the name of Jesus to cast out Satan, but they did not do it in the power of the Holy Spirit. The man who was possessed leaped on them, stripped off their clothes and made them run through the streets wounded and naked.

There is no power in the name of Jesus without the power of the Holy Spirit. But if we are filled with the quickening power of God, we can command the devil and he must go.

We must yield every day to that power and respond to that power so the quickening power of God flows through our bodies as a clear channel. Then, we can do great exploits for God. Then we can have a victorious experience every day of our lives.

Work Hard

God wants us to work hard. Titus 3:8 says "These things I will that thou affirm constantly, that they which have believed in God might be careful to maintain good works." God wants us to do a good job whether we are a factory worker, a housewife, a doctor, a preacher or a public school teacher.

The Holy Spirit quickens us in such a way that He can help us get out of bed every day eager for an exciting day. He can help us be at work 15 minutes early and then help us do an excellent job. He helps us to reach our full potential and to utilize every talent we have for the Lord. God's Word affirms that we must maintain good works. This can only be accomplished by the quickening power of the Holy Spirit.

Thinking Positively

Our minds are like computers. If we program our minds with negative thoughts, we will be defeated and discouraged. But if we program our minds to think victory, abundance, health and prosperity, that is what we will experience.

Philippians 4:8 says, "Whatsoever things are true, whatsoever things are honest, whatsoever things are just, whatsoever things are pure, whatsoever things are lovely, whatsoever things are of good report; if there be any virtue, and if there be any praise, think on these things."

As the Spirit flows through us constantly every day, we are going to think good thoughts, wholesome thoughts, beautiful thoughts that will produce victory in every area of our lives.

But the only way we will be able to experience this is as the Holy Spirit supplies faith. Faith, of course, comes directly from the Spirit of God. It does not find its source in us. The source of all faith is Jesus. The faith reaches us by the power of the Spirit of Christ through the Word.

In the same way that the Word sparks faith, negative thoughts feed the evil spirits that want to constantly torment us and keep us discouraged. A story about some ducks who live in the lake behind where I live will prove my point.

Not long ago I was pacing the seawall along the lake memorizing scripture. I noticed 11 wild ducks waddling behind me in a neat row on the seawall. My wife, Joyce, had apparently been feeding them, and they must have expected a handout from me.

I ignored them and walked to a lawn chair where I could read my Bible. They followed me as if we were playing "follow the leader." They formed a straight line about four feet from my chair waiting for their goodies. I just looked at them. For several minutes we had a staredown. Finally, the lead duck sensed I wasn't going to feed them. He began waddling toward the lake, and the others followed.

That's like Satan. If we feed him on negative thoughts, he and his imps from hell will stay around. If we starve him out, he will finally leave us alone.

Stay Full of the Spirit

We must be energized by the Holy Spirit if we are to please God. This must be a continual process. Ephesians 5:18 says, "And be not drunk with wine, wherein is excess; but be filled with the Spirit." The original Greek says "be ye being filled" with the Spirit. God wants us to have the Holy Spirit without measure. When we do, we'll be quickened in every area of our lives — whether we are working, going to school, relaxing or witnessing.

The Holy Spirit is the Spirit of righteousness. If we try to be righteous without the Holy Spirit quickening us, it is going to be our own righteousness. Isaiah 64:6 says that our righteousnesses are nothing but filthy rags. But when the Holy Spirit flows through our lives, then that is pleasing to God. That is what will gain us entrance to the portals of glory. We must have it. Without it we are lost.

Let's picture two glasses of water which represent two Christians — one charismatic and the other a non-charismatic. Both glasses are full, but the one representing the charismatic is full to running over. This would be the power of God overflowing in his life.

Now, let's suppose that the charismatic Christian does not replenish his supply each day, but the non-charismatic keeps his glass full — even though it doesn't overflow. Soon, he'll have a greater measure of the Spirit of God in his life than the charismatic who failed to replenish his supply. This is why many non-charismatic Christians can have a greater measure of the power of God in their lives than charismatics who do not replenish their supply daily. Remember, the command is still there: "be ye being filled."

Give Liberally

God wants us to give, but He wants us to give through the energy of the Holy Spirit. Proverbs 3:9, 10 says, "Honor the Lord with thy substance, and with the firstfruits of all thine increase: So shall thy barns be filled with plenty, and thy presses shall burst out with new wine."

Yet it may surprise you that I believe it is possible to outgive God. This happens when we go above and beyond the Holy Spirit — above and beyond faith. Then giving becomes tempting God.

Many people hear messages on faith without knowing all the ramifications. They don't realize their giving must be through the power of the Holy Spirit. They run away with the faith message, get themselves out on a limb financially, and are devastated when the limb is cut off under them.

Faith must grow gradually, like a plant. If you are

going to believe God for $1 million, start by believing Him for $10. If you want to go on a 40-day fast, go on a one-day fast first. Then, six months later, try a three-day fast. A year after that, take a 10-day fast and work up to a 40-day fast over a period of several years. Let your faith grow, otherwise you are going to get ahead of God and start tempting Him.

Jesus could have thrown himself off the pinnacle of the temple if He had wanted to. If God had been in it, He would have spared Jesus' life just as He spared it when He walked on the water. If we don't have the quickening power of the Holy Spirit to give us faith for whatever we want, we will be in a position of tempting God. God wants us to give liberally but to give in faith, in simplicity of the quickening power of the Holy Spirit. Then, He promises to reward us.

When giving is done in the right spirit, through the power of the Holy Spirit, it brings beautiful results. For example, I recently challenged the young couples in our congregation to tithe on what they would like to be making.

A young couple in the church who had several small children and were struggling to put the husband through his final year of college felt this quickened to their spirits. They decided this was for them, and they took the challenge.

They figured the amount they needed to feed and clothe their family and meet all their other obligations. They made out a check for tithes on that amount, prayed over that offering and put it in the collection plate.

The wife was a legal secretary. Within days she received a raise, then a bonus, then another raise. The husband worked as a cabinetmaker to put himself through college. Soon he had more orders than he could fill. Soon after that, their German Shepherd had pups. They sold all nine puppies for $150 each. God certainly met their need and honored their faith because they gave under the quickening power of the Holy Spirit.

Love Freely

God wants us to love freely. But there is no way to love your enemies, nor even Christians, without the quickening power of the Holy Spirit. This love must be quickened or energized to our hearts by the Holy Spirit. Then, we can love everybody. We will have animosity toward no one when we are filled with the quickening power of the Holy Spirit.

Jesus said in John 13:34, 35, "A new commandment I give unto you that ye love one another; as I have loved you, that ye also love one another. By this shall all men know that ye are my disciples, if ye have love one to another." In other words, we know that we are disciples of Christ if we have that quickening power of God to aid us in loving the unlovely.

Loving people means we must *like* them, too. Before the Roman Catholic Church began to experience the charismatic renewal, I loved Catholics in an obligatory way, but I did not like them. That was probably because the Catholics I knew acted as if they didn't like me. But attending one of the early charismatic meetings at Notre Dame changed all that for me.

From the moment I stepped on the campus in South Bend, Indiana, I could tell something was different. The only time I had been at the stadium before was for a football game with its carnival-like atmosphere.

At the charismatic meeting, however, there was praising God, real joy and a revival happiness that was contagious.

It was almost more than I could comprehend. A large sign proclaimed "Jesus Is Lord!" I saw thousands of Catholics with hands raised in worship singing songs of praise to the Lord. Rather than feeling as if Catholics didn't like me, it seemed everyone I met wanted to hug me. Before long I could not help laughing, crying and joining in their love for God and for one another. Now, I not only love Catholics, I *like* them.

Growing Consistently

Ephesians 4:15 tells us to grow consistently, that you may "grow up into Him in all things, which is the head, even Christ." The only way to grow is through the quickening power of the Holy Spirit.

How else can a Christian grow? No way. If we don't have the flow of the Holy Spirit, then we are going to be stunted in our growth. The only way to produce fruit and grow is by the quickening power of the Holy Spirit.

I have in my congregation Sister Elva Stump, a dear saint of God who is 93 years *young*. She went to Israel with us three years ago and she was more active than many people decades younger than she.

She is a vibrant, happy Christian who is seldom even sick. The reason she is like this is that she has never stopped growing.

I believe many older people who suffer one sickness after another and who become bitter and unhappy are like that because they fail to continue growing, learning and expanding their horizons. They, like us, should (as the Bible puts it) "go from one glory into another."

Forgive Everyone

This is a hard one. Yet God's Word says in Ephesians 4:32 to forgive everyone. But how do we forgive someone who has molested our daughter or killed our son? How can we forgive someone who has ridiculed us in public. We can't except by the power of the Holy Spirit.

When we refuse to forgive, we are usually the ones who suffer most. Unforgiveness is a terrible disease that can eat at us until we are bitter, unhappy people. Sometimes we can hold something against someone when that person didn't even *do* anything against us, but has just done something that made us jealous. If we have allowed resentment to creep into our lives, the best way to get rid of it is to go to the person and ask his forgiveness.

A pastor in a nearby city came by my office to see me recently. He walked into the room, stood in the center of the floor and wept convulsively. I thought perhaps his wife had been killed in an accident or his church had forced his resignation.

Finally he was able to control his sobs enough to ask me to forgive him. I told him I'd forgive him, but

I didn't know why.

"Because of this awful jealousy I have against you," he sobbed.

He finally explained that since our church had started a radio station, jealousy had been eating him like a cancer. It even affected his ability to minister effectively to his congregation. He had come to ask my forgiveness to get this terrible load off his shoulders.

Of course I forgave him. Today I have an excellent relationship with this man. I admire the courage he had to muster to come to me. It takes a mighty big man to do what he did. I know he relied on the Holy Spirit.

Witness to Everyone

Matthew 5:16 says to "Let your light so shine before men, that they may see your good works, and glorify your Father which is in heaven." I believe 95 per cent of all witnessing should be with out lives. The other five per cent should be verbal witnessing. Either way, witnessing must be done by the power of God.

Not long after I was saved, I had the opportunity to lead my two younger nephews to the Lord. I was a zealous young teenager and I loved to talk to everyone about Jesus. One summer I was working for my brother-in-law, their dad, shocking oats in a hayfield. My two nephews — Bruce, 9, and Robert, 12 — worked with me.

I asked the boys if they had ever been saved. They had grown up in church, but never had given their hearts to the Lord. They looked at each other, then at me. Finally, each shook his head no. They indicated that they would like to. So we knelt in the hayfield and prayed.

Those boys are men now, and each points to that experience in the hayfield as his conversion experience. Both are serving God today; one is in the ministry.

The Holy Spirit had been convicting the boys' hearts already. It wasn't just what I said that caused them to accept Jesus. But I had been living a consistent Christian life before them. If I hadn't, they would probably never have allowed me to lead them to Christ.

When we witness, it is so important to live what we are saying, not just mouthing the words.

He Quickens Us In The Resurrection

The Holy Spirit not only quickens us in this life, but he will quicken us in the resurrection when Christ returns to take his bride, the church, home. Paul describes what will happen this way: "The Lord Himself shall descend from heaven with a shout, with the voice of the archangel, and the trump of God: and the dead in Christ shall rise first: then we which are alive and remain shall be caught up together with them in the clouds, to meet the Lord in the air: and so shall we ever be with the Lord" (I Thes. 4:16, 17).

Isn't that exciting?

Someday we won't be subject to the same sicknesses, problems and frailties of being human. The Bible says that corruption will put on incorruption. Mortality will put on immortality. We will all be changed instantly, in the twinkling of an eye. Through the power of God, we will be changed to have the resurrection body of our Lord.

This new body will be more marvelous than anything science fiction writers could have imagined. We will be able to commute back and forth between heaven and earth. We will be able to appear and disappear. We will travel as fast as the speed of light from one place on earth to another, after we return with Christ to rule and reign for 1,000 years.

God's plan for us is to come back with Christ in the Battle of Armageddon. We will be a part of that great invasion in which all the armies of Anti-Christ, and all the foes of Christ will be defeated.

That will initiate the thousand years of peace. The curse of Satan will be broken; he will be thrown into the bottomless pit. All the world will know who Jesus Christ is. In fact, He will rule the inhabitants of earth with a rod of iron. The wonderful thing is that we will be here with Him ruling and reigning, too.

Paul looked forward to that day, just as we do, in which the Holy Spirit will quicken all believers in the resurrection. Read what he says about it in Romans 8:15-19:

"For ye have not received the spirit of bondage again to fear; but ye have received the Spirit of adoption, whereby we cry, Abba, Father. The Spirit itself beareth witness with our spirit, that we are the children of God: And if children, then heirs; heirs of God, and joint-heirs with Christ; if so be that we suffer with him, that we may be also glorified together.

"For I reckon that the sufferings of this present time are not worthy to be compared with the glory which shall be revealed in us. For the earnest expectation of the creature waiteth for the manifestation of the sons of God."

One of these days, it may be at noon, or at night, or in the morning, Jesus Christ will appear to every Christian as He comes for us in the clouds. Gravity will lose its force. Our bodies will be changed in a moment. We will be caught up to meet the Lord in the air. He will take us to heaven along with everyone else who is "in Christ," even those who have died who have known Him. All will be quickened by the Holy Spirit.

Oh, to be in that number; to be counted with the faithful; to be ready for that day!

Lord, Jesus, help all of us to be ready!

Epilogue

What about your soul? Have you experienced the power of God? Are you born again? If you are not, you can be. You have read this far, so the Holy Spirit must be dealing with your heart. Right now, you can receive the Spirit of Jesus, who is the power of God into your innermost being. Then, you can know beyond a shadow of a doubt that if you died today that you would spend eternity in heaven.

I invite you to pray this simple prayer:

"Lord Jesus, I am sorry for the way I have tried to live without You. Forgive me of everything wrong I've ever done — for all the sin I've committed. I know it's displeasing to You.

"Jesus, I invite You to enter my life now, way down deep in my soul. Blend Your wonderful Spirit with my spirit. Make me alive spiritually. I accept You now, Jesus. Come into my life. I trust in You as my Savior, my Lord, my soon-coming King, and my God.

"Thank you, Father, for letting Your Son, Jesus,

MOUNTAIN-MOVING MOTIVATION

by His Spirit, come into me. Thank You right now for saving my soul! Amen."

If you prayed that prayer and meant it, then you are forgiven! The Word of God promises you eternal life when you turn your life over to Jesus. You have just been born again! Now, begin praising God. Worship Him. Open up to His presence that you feel in your spirit.

What you are sensing right now is the power of God!

The Story of First Assembly

For years, First Assembly of God in Lakeland, Florida, has been one of the great churches in its denomination. It has had several great pastors including J. Foy Johnson, who resigned in 1966 after pastoring 13 years to become District Superintendent of the Peninsular Florida District of the Assemblies of God.

The congregation called as its new pastor a 37-year-old minister from South Bend, Indiana — Karl D. Strader. The church was already a strong, established congregation, averaging 325 on Sunday in a building seating 750. When he came to Lakeland, Pastor Strader found the congregation "ready to go."

As Pastor Strader preached the Word of God, marvelous things began to happen. Scores of visitors began to come and were saved and filled with the Holy Spirit. The congregation continued to grow spiritually. People flocked to First Assembly to see what was happening. Many stayed. Soon double

Sunday services were necessary to hold the crowds.

A Monday night "charismatic service" was added for denominational friends who wanted to learn about the work of the Holy Spirit. As the people of First Assembly welcomed them without compromising their own Assemblies of God witness, the church began to take on a "transdenominational" atmosphere.

Pastor Strader's wife, Joyce, has conducted a charismatic Outreach program for women since 1971. The purpose is to expose every woman in Lakeland to the pentecostal experience. Thousands of new women throughout the Central Florida area have attended these monthly Saturday Outreach luncheons. Hundreds have received the Baptism in the Holy Spirit. Hundreds of others have been saved, delivered from evil spirits and healed by the power of God.

First Assembly has always reached out to others outside its own four walls. World Missions giving is emphasized. Last year, for example, the church gave more than $350,000 to foreign and home missions. As the people have given to God, He has blessed them financially. In 1966, annual revenues were $55,000. Last year, it was more than $1 million. This growth has allowed the ministry of First Assembly to expand. Today it includes:

WCIE. This 50,000-watt FM radio station (91.3 on the dial) reaches more than 100,000 listeners each week in the Central Florida area. The format ranges from country gospel music in the morning, to contemporary Christian music in the afternoon, to easy-listening Christian music at night.

Programs include those from well-known Bible teachers, talk shows, news, weather, sports, tips for homemakers, and "Time to Live" three times daily, a 15-minute program by Pastor Strader. The call letters — WCIE — stand for "Where Christ Is Everything." Broadcast studios are located at First Assembly.

Television ministry. A 10-minute daily telecast called "New Day," shown on Channel 8, WFLA-TV in Tampa, Florida, reaches more than 30,000 viewers each morning. The program features the host, Jim Campbell, with a scripture, a song by talented singers and musicians in the church, and a devotional by Pastor Strader. It is filmed at First Assembly.

In addition, all services at First Assembly are filmed and shown on a cablevision channel in Lakeland. The church provides 10-and-a-half hours daily on cable, including other Christian programs such as the "PTL Club", the "700 Club" and Oral Roberts' program, on the cablevision channel. The Sunday morning services are taped and aired for prime time on Channel 51 in the Miami area. The PTL satellite transmits several First Assembly programs to 100 stations around the country. The programs are also shipped to stations as far away as the Samoan Islands.

The First Assembly Ministries mobile television unit tapes television programs for Gerald Derstine and Vep Ellis, programs for the Assemblies of God Foreign Missions Department, and several other local churches.

A team of counselors answers the phones from 7 p.m. to 11 p.m. each night and pray for those who call in who have been listening to WCIE or watching the programs on the cablevision channel in Lakeland.

Evangel Christian School. More than 600 children from nursery through 12th grade are taught at First Assembly. Some children are bussed from as far away as 20 miles. More than 40 percent of the children come from families representing many other denominations.

Dayspring. This is the youth ministry of First Assembly which involves hundreds of teenagers in active programs which contribute to a real family emphasis in the church.

Royal Rangers and Missionettes. These are two highly successful denominational programs for boys and girls respectively. The programs are somewhat like Boy Scouts and Girl Scouts, only with a decidedly Christian emphasis.

Adult Singles Group. This was one of the first groups in the nation organized in a local church to minister specifically to young adult singles — especially the divorced and widowed. The group has helped scores of people to develop meaningful relationships with others, and to enhance their own spiritual growth.

Senior Citizens. Lakeland is a popular retirement area, and many of these people call First Assembly their church home. There are several prayer meetings at the church each week which are well attended by senior citizens who are free during the day. There are also covered-dish dinners and other functions.

Other ministries include Women's Ministries, Men's Ministries, and a counseling department which helps scores of people each week.

Today, with the radio/tv outreaches, an estimated 5,000 people in Central Florida call First Assembly their church home. The tremendous growth required the congregation to build a beautiful new auditorium seating 1,850 back in 1974. Later, they built a modern gymnasium and classrooms nearby. The old auditorium was remodeled into classrooms by adding a second floor. Plans are on the drawing boards for a new sanctuary seating 6,000 to 10,000.

Now with its 13 pastors, including Jim Campbell, Allen Trimble, Tom Hartshorn, Lloyd Wead, Buddy McCormick, Shelby Lanier, Bobby Leverette, David Thomas, Steve Strader, Mark Hurst, Randy Helms, Crandall Miller, Gary Cook and Business Manager Joe Perez, First Assembly is a happy, positive church. The goodness of God is emphasized in the services. The people are excited about learning about God. They bring their Bibles and take notes during the sermons.

But the most wonderful thing about First Assembly is the love that is shown. You can see it on the faces of the people as they arrive; you can sense it as soon as you enter the parking lot. The people are warm and friendly. The services are powerful and exciting. When you visit, you just know that "God is in this place."

photo by Jim Ferrell

First Assembly's handsome new sanctuary seating 1,850, as seen from the ground and from the air (left page). Notice the original sanctuary in the extreme right in the lower photo.

People raise their hands in worship as Associate Pastor Jim Campbell leads a chorus in a Sunday service. (above) Pastor Strader is on the platform in the black suit. At right is a close-up of Jim leading the singing as Bobby Leverette (whose face is just above the camera) and Tom Hartshorn (in the white suit in front of the camera) minister to those who came forward for prayer. First Assembly televises all its services.

Pastor Strader is excited when he preaches and he moves aro

124

photos by Jim Ferrell

his series of photos was taken in a recent service at First Assembly.

125

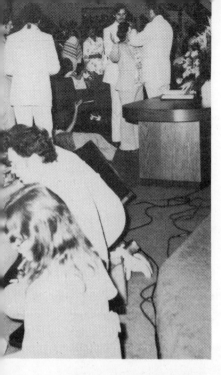

Left: Pastor Strader (in white suit in front of communion table at right) prays for a woman in a healing line at the end of a service at First Assembly. Prayer for the sick is an important part of the ministry of the church. Below: Pastor Strader (in dark suit in front of Bible) dedicates a baby during a service at First Assembly. This photo shows part of the vast congregation that packs the auditorium each service.

photos by Jim Ferrell

Joyce Wead Strader is an important part of Pastor Strader's ministry. Her vivacious personality and creative mind add much to the effectiveness of the church in reaching the area for Jesus. She founded an Outreach program for ladies in 1971 which reaches the women in the Lakeland, Florida, area with the pentecostal experience.

If you have accepted Jesus as a result of reading this book, if you came into a deeper experience with Jesus, or if you have questions about being a Christian, I will send you helpful literature if you write me and ask for it. Address your letters to:

Karl D. Strader
First Assembly of God
1350 E. Main Street
Lakeland, Florida 33801